More Praise for *The Revolution Where You Live*

"What the world needs today is a modern Odysseus—one who speaks with the power and love of the feminine, listens from the heart, and acts from compassion. Sarah van Gelder is that hero, a woman who understands that the monsters blocking our paths are our own creations, that the way out of chaos is through soul-felt, community-centered involvement. *The Revolution Where You Live* is a song of modern redemption."
—**John Perkins, *New York Times* bestselling author of *The New Confessions of an Economic Hit Man***

"What a journey! Sarah van Gelder uncovers the real revolution unfolding across America: leaderless and leader-full, up against it and angry, but still willing to hope. A passionate, powerful account!"
—**Bill McKibben, author of *Deep Economy* and *The End of Nature* and cofounder of 350.org**

"Journalist Sarah van Gelder says we can build the political revolution Bernie Sanders talks about from the bottom up, away from the iron grip of Wall Street and wealthy corporate interests. That's a future we can all believe in."
—**RoseAnn DeMoro, Executive Director, National Nurses United, and National Vice President, AFL-CIO**

"Slow food is a local, healthy homemade meal, prepared with a lot of love. Sister Sarah has a similar talent as she shares with us her snail ride across Turtle Island—not as a fable but as independent media evidence that decolonization and the Great Turning are here. We the people *love* this place!"
—**Pancho Ramos-Stierle, full-time ServiceSpace volunteer, Oakland, and undocumented and unafraid activist and meditator**

"This book will keep you warm even as it keeps you riveted, and it will inspire you to see your part in the solutions that our world so desperately needs."
—**Brendan Martin, founder and Director, The Working World**

"Buckminster Fuller reminded us that we are facing a civilizational choice between utopia and oblivion. In this intrepid account, Sarah van Gelder renders the realistic utopia possible and reminds us that it is being born, right now, in the heart of the old empire."
—**Alnoor Ladha, Executive Director, The Rules, and Board Member, Greenpeace International USA**

"Like the inspiring efforts that she chronicles, Sarah van Gelder's writing is 'ordinary and extraordinary.' In sharp contrast to mass media blather and clichés of condescension, this book offers hope grounded in real human experience."
—**Norman Solomon, Executive Director, Institute for Public Accuracy, and author of** *War Made Easy*

"People are hungry for solutions, and those that unfold in these beautifully told stories offer hope and ways to build bridges of justice and understanding."
—**LeeAnn Hall, Co–Executive Director, People's Action**

"This is a wonderful book—warm, human, direct, meaningful—and it is one that will help you understand why building a new America from the ground up must begin with community."
—**Gar Alperovitz, author of** *What Then Must We Do?*

"In this good book, Sarah van Gelder documents her reprise of Alexis de Tocqueville's 1831 travels in search of democracy. It is a book of answers: homegrown, walking-distance, smart, and heartfelt."
—**Peter Block, author of** *Community*

"Our survival depends today on rediscovering hope as a social force. This is what Sarah van Gelder does in this amazing book, where she shares sources of hope that she collected with love and wisdom."
—**Gustavo Esteva, writer, speaker, and founder of Universidad de la Tierra**

"Bravo! Through masterful storytelling, Sarah van Gelder shares a critical insight—that when we connect to the place where we live and work in community, we have the power to overcome the complex challenges of our time."
—**Judy Wicks, cofounder of Business Alliance for Local Living Economies and author of** *Good Morning, Beautiful Business*

"Sarah van Gelder's genius, in the spirit of Wendell Berry, is to celebrate the women, men, and children who cultivate love for their places in all their diversity. This book inspires us to regenerate our connections with each other and to the ecology of our place on earth."
—**Madhu S. Prakash, author and Professor of Education, Penn State College of Education**

The Revolution Where You Live

The Revolution Where You Live

Stories from a 12,000-Mile Journey through a New America

Sarah van Gelder

Foreword by Danny Glover

BK

Berrett–Koehler Publishers, Inc.
a BK Currents book

Berrett-Koehler Publishers, Inc.
1333 Broadway, Suite 1000
Oakland, CA 94612-1921
Tel: (510) 817-2277   Fax: (510) 817-2278   www.bkconnection.com

Ordering Information

Quantity sales. Special discounts are available on quantity purchases by corporations, associations, and others. For details, contact the "Special Sales Department" at the Berrett-Koehler address above.

Individual sales. Berrett-Koehler publications are available through most bookstores. They can also be ordered directly from Berrett-Koehler: Tel: (800) 929-2929; Fax: (802) 864-7626; www.bkconnection.com

Orders for college textbook/course adoption use. Please contact Berrett-Koehler: Tel: (800) 929-2929; Fax (802) 864-7626.

Orders by U.S. trade bookstores and wholesalers. Please contact Ingram Publisher Services, Tel: (800) 509-4887; Fax (800) 838-1149; E-mail: customer.service@ingrampublisherservices.com; or visit www.ingrampublisherservices.com/Ordering for details about electronic ordering.

Berrett-Koehler and the BK logo are registered trademarks of Berrett-Koehler Publishers, Inc.

Printed in the United States of America

Berrett-Koehler books are printed on long-lasting acid-free paper. When it is available, we choose paper that has been manufactured by environmentally responsible processes. These may include using trees grown in sustainable forests, incorporating recycled paper, minimizing chlorine in bleaching, or recycling the energy produced at the paper mill.

Cataloging data is available from the Library of Congress, catalog no. 2016037986

ISBN: 978-1-62656-765-8

First Edition
21 20 19 18 17   10 9 8 7 6 5 4 3 2 1

Front cover, top (left to right): detail from mural at Growing Power Chicago; George Price, permaculture farmer and professor; detail from mural in Newark, New Jersey; Jewell Praying Wolf James, carver, Lummi Tribe.

Photo of author on cover by Paul Dunn. All other cover and interior photos by Sarah van Gelder unless otherwise noted.

Maps by Evan Winslow Smith

Produced by Wilsted & Taylor Publishing Services
    Copyediting by Melody Lacina   Design and composition by Nancy Koerner

To my partner, Dee Axelrod,

who supported my wild idea

of a four-and-a-half-month solo road trip,

then gave me writing solitude

when I needed it and feedback on the ideas

and writing when I needed that—

and if that wasn't enough,

she agreed to marry me

Contents

I. Setting Out, from the North/Northwest

II. The Midwest

III. The East

IV. Home, via Texas and the Southwest

Foreword

In a speech delivered at Manhattan's Riverside
Church in April 1967, Dr. Martin Luther King Jr. stated:

> We are now faced with the fact that tomorrow is today. We
> are confronted with the fierce urgency of now. In this un-
> folding conundrum of life and history there is such a thing
> as being too late. Procrastination is still the thief of time. Life
> often leaves us standing bare, naked and dejected with a lost
> opportunity. . . . This may well be mankind's last chance to
> choose between chaos or community.

We live in a world in which chaos seems to be winning out:
police shootings of unarmed black men and women, war
abroad and in our streets, the devastating impacts of climate
change, the hardships faced by millions of Americans struggling to feed their families and make ends meet. Yet Dr. King
stated that we have a choice—we can choose community. But
what does community mean in this moment in history? As a
starting point, it means that we reimagine our relationships to
one another and to the natural world. This book, written by

Sarah van Gelder, tells the stories of people around the United States who are reimaging the world around them and, in doing so, creating new possibilities for community. Sarah spent nearly five months traveling 12,000 miles around the United States, learning how people are creating a revolution right where they live. She visited Native American reservations that—in spite of their historic social and economic struggles as stewards of the planet Earth—are blocking attempts by fossil fuel companies to mine coal and engage in fracking for oil and gas. Sarah visited Chicago, Detroit, Cincinnati, and small towns in Appalachia and New Mexico, learning from people working to create just and locally rooted economies. She visited leaders in Greensboro, North Carolina; Harrisonburg, Virginia; Ithaca, New York; and Moab, Utah, who are building bridges of justice and understanding between divided communities.

When I travel the world as a UNICEF Goodwill ambassador, I see time and time again the essential role of communities. It is people working locally, joining together to create powerful movements of resistance and reimagining what's possible that gives me hope. In the United States, it is in local communities that we see the impact of toxic pollution, poverty, and poor schools, which together create the world's highest rates of incarceration. But it is also in communities that we see people working to protect and restore water quality, stepping up to create safe and liberating spaces for children to learn, and reaching out to the formerly incarcerated to welcome them home.

It is in community that we can stop the environmental pollution that causes children in South Central Los Angeles to have a third of the lung capacity as children in Santa Monica. And it is in intergenerational communities that children can learn from their elders to master the tools needed to live intelligent, creative, and involved lives. Even the global movement to prevent climate disruption and resist projects like the KXL pipeline are most powerful when they are based in the communities most affected.

Paul Robeson once said that each generation defines its own history. We, too, will be defined by the history we make. Like Robeson, we live in a time of crisis. It is a time of racial injustice, poverty, war, and irreparable damage done to nature. It is a time of growing divides between the wealthy and the poor, and a time when the working class struggles to hold on to what they have. Those crises test who we are as people.

> Our goal is to create a beloved community and this will require a qualitative change in our souls as well as a quantitative change in our lives.

Those are the words of Dr. King. It is in reimaging our relationships to each other and to nature that we make the sort of change Dr. King advocated, a change centered in our souls. This book tells the stories of people stepping up to make soul-centered changes. Often these local actions are not dramatic, and no one has all the answers. But each of us has something to offer, and in reading about the people Sarah interviewed and in learning of the changes they are bringing about, it becomes clearer that the chaos of the early twenty-first century is just part of the story. The community Dr. King spoke of is also a possibility for the human future, and in neighborhoods, reservations, small towns, and struggling cities, people are working every day to make that possibility a reality. That is a deeply hopeful sign that the beloved community Dr. King spoke of may, after all, be the legacy we leave our children.

DANNY GLOVER
San Francisco

A Big Revolution at a Small Scale

On August 15, 2015, I climbed into a 12-year-old, four-cylinder pickup truck and began an 18-week journey.

I drove 12,000 miles, starting at home, in Suquamish, Washington, an Indian reservation just west of Seattle, and visited 18 states, five Indian reservations, five industrial cities, and a smattering of small towns.

I camped on a mountaintop in the Kentucky coalfields and stopped in at the renowned Highlander Center in New Market, Tennessee, where Rosa Parks and Martin Luther King Jr. came to talk strategy, and where Pete Seeger cowrote "We Shall Overcome." I visited Native American pueblos of northern New Mexico; I camped on a ranch in Montana, by Lake Erie in Ohio, and in a canyon outside Amarillo, Texas. People invited me to sleep in their spare rooms, and when I got snowed in, I stayed in a cheap hotel on the Idaho border with Oregon.

People I met on the road, *YES! Magazine* readers, and people who followed my blog tipped me off to good stories and introduced me to extraordinary people.

The reason for the trip? I wanted to find out what people

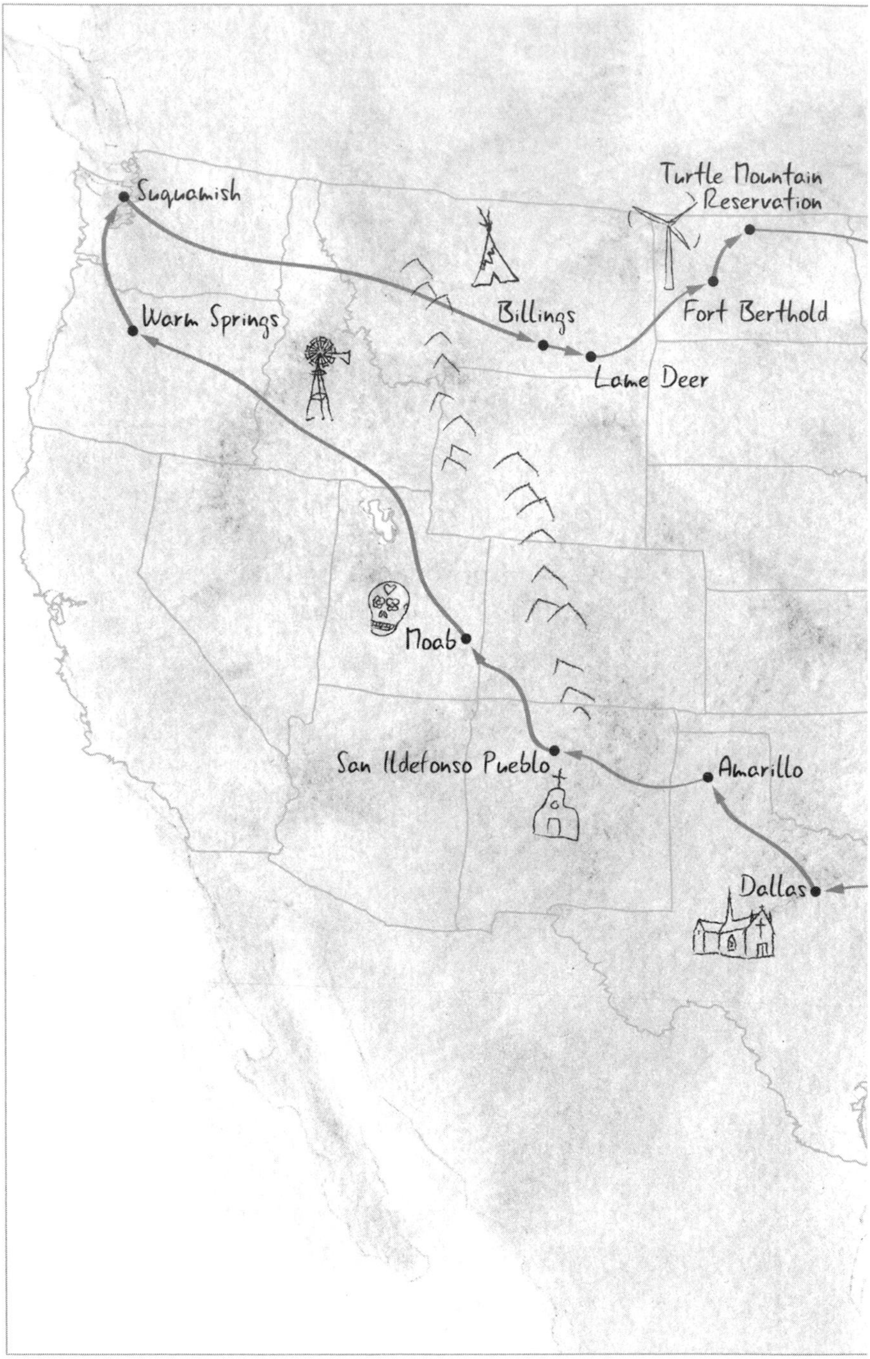
Suquamish
Turtle Mountain Reservation
Warm Springs
Billings
Fort Berthold
Lame Deer
Moab
San Ildefonso Pueblo
Amarillo
Dallas

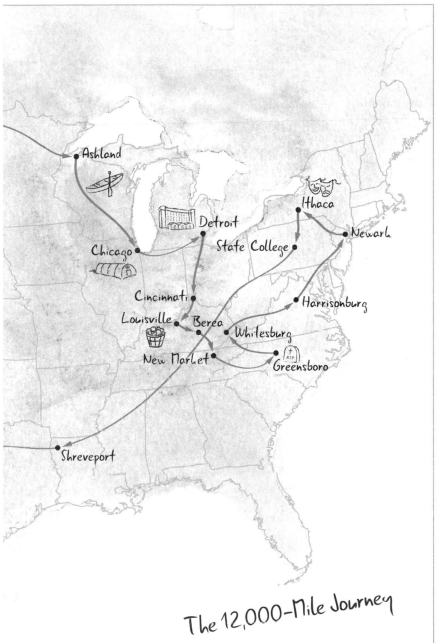

The 12,000-Mile Journey

are doing in their communities about poverty and inequality, the climate crisis, and racism. I especially wanted to find out if the places at the margins of society might have answers, and if those answers were early signs of a new society.

These are tough times. Fully half of Americans are poor,[1] while virtually all the economic gains since the 2008 economic crash have gone to a tiny elite. Isolation is making people depressed, sick, and powerless. The climate crisis is jeopardizing our future, and opportunistic politicians are whipping up racism and hate to win over voters angry about being locked out of the prosperity that others seem to enjoy.

The media keep us distracted with celebrity gossip and trivia, but they ignore the really big stories that will determine the sort of future we have.

I cofounded *YES! Magazine* 20 years ago to explore underreported stories that matter, particularly the stories that show how people are taking on some of the big crises of our time. If our current systems are failing—and I believe they are—then I wanted to look for evidence that people are creating a different sort of world.

We found lots of evidence as we researched the stories and issue themes, from the viral spread of local food to the national movement against mass incarceration. People around the United States and around the world are creating worker-owned cooperatives, urban farms, time banks, land trusts, and restorative justice circles. As they do that, they are also creating and finding more satisfying ways to live and leaving behind consumer values for things that matter more.

But is all this good work enough? In spite of well-crafted critiques, social movements, public opinion, and lots of hard work, inequality continues to grow; racism remains embedded in American culture; and there seems to be no way to stop big corporations from outsourcing our jobs, contaminating our water, soil, and air, and flooding media channels with distraction and lies. Especially worrisome is that we are running out of time to rein in the heating of the globe, which is happening even more rapidly than scientists feared.

I left on my road trip to find out if there is still hope. Are there solutions that are up to the challenges of our time, and if so, what forms do they take?

I traveled through Montana and North Dakota, where I found Native and ranching communities that have shut down fracking and mining—and are developing a restorative vision for their region. In the Rust Belt cities of the Midwest, I found people resisting home foreclosures and working to build a locally rooted economy with room for everyone. On the East Coast, I found people grappling with the nation's legacy of racism and taking steps to heal and bring justice. Throughout the country, I found people creating worker-owned enterprises, building bridges across race lines, regenerating the soil, and developing their own place-based economies.

In difficult times, strong-man leaders often arise who offer an outlet for anger, and fear disguised as nationalism.

On the left, too, revolutions often have larger-than-life leaders who mobilize millions. Those who are hungry for change may be excited by these powerful movements. But they tend to spawn authoritarian systems, and we have seen the disasters associated with patriarchal, top-down change.

The revolution I discovered is decentralized, far less flashy, and better able to include everyone, especially those now excluded from wealth and power. It doesn't rely on self-important leaders. It undercuts the values that have driven our consumer-based culture, the isolation that sickens the soul, the racism and the greed that drive Wall Street and corrupt their collaborators in government. Instead, it is about reclaiming our rights to what really matters—community, life, the healing and unfolding of each person, and the vitality and restoration of the natural world, including the threatened species with whom we share this Earth.

I came back from my travels believing that this sort of revolution is our only real hope in the face of ecological and social unraveling.

The only way such a big revolution can happen is, ironically, at a small scale. Only where we live, in our neighborhoods and cities and towns where we encounter each other and can know each other, can the transformation be deep enough. Only in community can we reconnect to each other, to the natural world, and to our own deepest values. That reconnection is our source of power and hope.

No charismatic leader or top-down revolution can bring about the needed change. Only by working together in the places we call home can we overcome isolation, embrace our differences, confront the extractive economy, and create the sort of world that will work for all of us, including nonhuman life.

We the People Love This Place

Where I began

As a seven-year-old child, I lived in India while my father was on exchange at a small university in Andhra Pradesh, and I've carried a question with me ever since. Why do we tolerate so much suffering? We humans are creative, brilliant, and inventive—why do we allow poverty?

The question arose from a particular event, although there were many similar moments during that year. One beautiful weekend day, my parents, my three sisters, and I set out in a borrowed jeep to a meadow on a hillside outside the city and spread out a blanket and a picnic.

It wasn't long before we realized we were being watched. Slowly, a small crowd of children had gathered. Some were my age, with baby sisters or brothers held on a hip. All were thin, wearing very little; all, we assumed, were hungry. They kept their distance—they just watched in a silent semicircle. Their steady gaze was impossible to ignore. The hard-boiled egg dried up in my mouth.

I understood something about suffering. Two years earlier, I had lost my mother, abruptly, to a stroke. Our family pulled together and cared for each other, but I entered an unfamiliar world then, just as I did when we moved to India.

I remember thinking, I don't understand this—I don't know why I should wake up every day knowing I have enough to eat and finish the day knowing I would have a safe place to sleep, when so many other children don't have those things. I remember thinking, I don't understand this now, but I won't forget, and when I grow up, I will do what I can to change this.

We didn't go on any more picnics, but those children stayed with me when I returned to the United States.

Some years later, living with my family in the Hudson Valley of New York State, I learned that my country, the country I pledged allegiance to every day in grade school, was conducting a brutal war on the people of Vietnam. I felt betrayed and, more importantly, deep grief and shame that we would inflict such harm on another people. And again, I felt some responsibility. This war was only possible because our family, like other American families, was paying for it with our taxes.

When I left college, I moved to Portland, Oregon, and arrived broke, knowing no one. I started working in the kitchen of a downtown restaurant. Later, I found a job in a tiny cooperative business that sold organic produce to Portland-area food co-ops. I was excited to be part of building a cooperative economy that was supplying fresh and nutritious food to co-op members, encouraging ecologically sound farming methods, and supporting farms that were not exploiting their workers. It felt great to be part of the solution.

Later, I traveled to Guatemala; as part of my preparation for the trip, I learned about President Jacobo Árbenz, a reformer who had instituted a moderate form of land reform intended to allow poor farmers and indigenous communities to farm and move out of poverty.[1] The United Fruit Company wasn't having it, though. In 1954, the United States helped to overthrow the democratically elected government, and big corporations were again free to extract the wealth of Guatemala; small farmers, deprived of fertile land and a say in government, were impoverished. Worse, the dictators propped up by the U.S. government conducted decades of brutal warfare against their own people, especially against indigenous communities. Those who protested turned up dead by the side of the road. Terror enforced inequity, and, I realized with shame, my country was enforcing the terror.

Out of these experiences grew my commitment to do what I could to address the fundamental causes of inequity and violence—and, later, environmental degradation.

At the root of these issues, I think, is a system of beliefs and a power structure that allow big corporations and their enablers in government to extract wealth from our natural world and our communities. A worldview that devalues people of color and turns their land, labor, and bodies into extractable resources is also part of the picture. Until recently, many white Americans believed they would benefit from this system of corporate capitalism, or at least be immune from its worst excesses. But big corporations and the neoliberal policies they endorse have undermined the foundations of the middle class and turned mountaintops, waterways, and urban neighborhoods in the United States into sacrifice zones. They've rolled over small businesses with big-box stores, our homes with predatory lending, our schools with privatization schemes, and our medical care with bloated drug costs. Plus, they've pushed on us foods laden with chemical additives, genetically modified organisms (GMOs), and antibiotics (which are creating resistant forms of diseases that may soon make routine ailments into life-threatening catastrophes).

To tolerate this, we learn to numb ourselves, binge watching television series, taking drugs, or overeating. We separate ourselves emotionally from our communities, from the natural world, even from ourselves. Schools teach us this, as does advertising.

We learn to accept the demise of beloved outdoor spaces and of wild species. Maybe our obsession with cute animal videos is an emotional compensation for the pain of losing the diverse life forms that wink out on a daily basis.

We learn to leave family or community to chase down a better job, to leave our children in sterile child-care centers because we have to earn a few dollars working a low-wage job. We learn from watching nonstop images of violence in the media that other people are not trustworthy.

And we learn to use stuff to fill the hole left by isolation and to disassociate from our deepest values. We adopt the values of consumerism and learn to live vicariously via celebrities and to accept the illnesses that come from stress, toxins, and bad food.

I'm not sure why we allow all this. I think it must be because we are exhausted by trying to get by—many people are deep in debt and work multiple jobs to pay the rent. And we are mesmerized by corporate media. And we are isolated.

When we lose our connections to each other, we lose our power. We believe we can't change things and can't remake our world. We lose the ability to create an economy together, and we become dependent on big corporations for our livelihoods. And we become less able to resist advertising messages that tell us we are only worthy if we buy stuff. Our isolation, when coupled with economic hardship, makes us vulnerable to the hate speech of demagogues.

When we disconnect from the natural world, we lose a grounding, a sense of belonging to a larger community of life, as well as an experience of the wildness and freedom we share with our cousins of other species.

Building a community and a magazine

There are ways people can reconnect, though, even if society as a whole is fragmenting. When my husband and I started a family, we chose to raise our young children in a community we helped to form on Bainbridge Island, Washington, a short ferry ride from Seattle.

I remember a moment in 1991, when a group of some 15 of us looked around the circle at each other, took a collective deep breath, and committed to continue with the long meetings, difficult interpersonal issues, and financial risks in order to build a cohousing community.

We had five acres of land, the inspiration of Danish cohousing communities, and architectural drawings. Our plan was 30 small homes, mostly in duplexes, clustered close together. A parking lot in the corner would be the only area to accommodate cars. The remainder of the site would be for a common house, a large organic garden, an orchard, a pond, and a play field. Making the housing small and tightly clustered would keep the homes affordable and allow us to save open space for play, gardening, and nature.

The other thing we had was our belief in each other, a belief honed by many months spent working to bring this vision to reality.

What we didn't have was financing. We were facing the prospect of losing all the time and money we had invested because we couldn't find a bank that would loan us money to construct the project. At this critical meeting, we had to decide whether to put in more of our own money, or cut our losses and go home.

We took the leap.

Not long after, a credit union came forward with the financing. "You're not that different from us," the president told us. "You are owned by your members—we're owned by ours." With their loan, our cooperative community was built, and a year later, we moved into one of the first cohousing communities in the United States.

The experience of living there was ordinary and extraordinary. Everyday life included the usual work of raising a family, plus additional obligations to co-manage the land, buildings, finances, and group dynamics of nearly 100 people. But it was also extraordinary. When someone was ill, or dying, the community surrounded them with love and help. When babies were born, we supported the family and shared the delight.

On the twentieth anniversary of the founding of the community, a group of confident, thriving young adults—whose earliest memories were of playing in the common house and woods and gardens—came back to share what it meant to them to grow up with the support of a loving community. Many who live their lives in traditional villages take this sort of support for granted. Yet in the world's wealthiest country, this simple community connection can be difficult to find or to create.

In 1996, we founded *YES! Magazine.* Like many startups, we had an energized small team, an idea we thought important, and a basement for our offices. But unlike many startups, we had no money, so the early years were difficult.

Still, we found that people were hungry for the sort of solutions stories we produced in *YES!* They wanted to know that a better way was possible. The questions I'd lived with all my life—how can we end poverty, inequality, violence, and environmental harm, and build a world that works for all people and all life—were questions we asked every day. And we spent our time researching and reporting on the people around the country and around the world who were creating answers—often in their own communities.

Reporting on the answers helped them to spread as others picked up the ideas. Magazine themes, which included multiple angles on a topic, revealed something even more profound. These innovations formed something larger than individual stories of change; together they revealed the outline of a possible new world in the making.

Understanding my place, or trying to

Today I live on the Port Madison Indian Reservation across Puget Sound from Seattle, a place that, as a non-Native, I can never really call mine. The events since I moved here in the year 2000 have changed me, giving me a glimpse of an indigenous perspective on place, the natural world, how people once lived without police, and the role of elders and women. And living here has made me think deeply about racism and poverty, and about community-based transformation.

In 2000, I bought a small cabin on a quiet street in Suquamish, a small town on the Port Madison Indian Reservation. Suquamish is on the waterfront, looking east across Puget Sound toward Seattle. It's a checkerboard reservation, made up of land owned by the tribe, Native American families, and non-Natives. Once I knew I'd be living here, I visited the tribal museum to learn about this community.

When Chief Seattle was alive, I learned, a giant longhouse, more than 600 feet long, made out of split cedar logs and hand-carved poles, was his home and the home of many others, and the center of the tribe's main village. People would come in canoes from all over the region and spend days at a stretch at Old Man House, as it was called, in potlatches and other ceremonies.

The U.S. government–appointed Indian agent ordered the longhouse burned down shortly after Chief Seattle died in 1866. When word reached Angeline, Chief Seattle's daughter, she paddled her canoe the 13 miles across Puget Sound from Seattle; according to the story, she arrived weeping, crying, "They're burning down Papa's home," and scooping water from Puget Sound with her hands to pour on the dying embers.

The people rebuilt separate homes and a church on the same piece of land. But in 1904, the military informed the tribe that it would be taking almost the entire waterfront to build fortifications to protect the nearby Bremerton Navy shipyards. The people were paid a token fee and moved off of the ancestral waterfront land, a segment of the small reservation they had retained as part of the Treaty of Point Elliott when they relinquished the land where the city of Seattle now sits.

The military never did use the land for fortifications to protect the shipyards. Instead, it sold the ground to developers who subdivided it for vacation homes. The state of Washington, recognizing the historic importance of the land where Old Man House had stood, bought three of those lots and turned them into a state park. About a mile away, my house stands back from the waterfront, among the trees, on a section of another of those lots.

A reluctant activist

Many of us know in a sort of general way that the land we live on was taken from an indigenous nation. I know the specifics. When I visited the tribe's museum and saw the map, I thought that if there ever came a time when the tribe wanted to get back their stolen land, I would work with them.

Still, when I first moved there, I had no intention of stirring things up. I was in the intense early years of getting *YES! Magazine* off the ground, and I was raising two children, so I wasn't looking for a project. Also, I am deeply skeptical that well-meaning outsiders can move into a community and do good—especially a white outsider moving into a community of color.

But one day, one of my neighbors knocked on my door and invited me to join others in opposition to the tribe's plan to build housing in our mainly white neighborhood. At a big community meeting, non-Native residents of the reservation, one after another, stood up to tell the county commissioner that they didn't want "those people" living nearby. The tone got more hostile as the evening wore on.

I was paralyzed by confusion. I hadn't realized I was living in the midst of this anti-Indian hostility, and I had come to the meeting alone; I knew almost no one. Finally, though, I couldn't stay silent, and I spoke up for the right of the tribe to house their members on their reservation. One or two people applauded, but clearly I had violated the script—the flier that announced the meeting called on us to stay united against the tribe.

As I left the meeting, an older man followed me outside and introduced himself. His name was Ted George, he told me. I realized to my horror that this soft-spoken Native elder had witnessed 90 minutes of anti-Indian speeches, which were continuing inside the building. He thanked me for speaking up, we talked for a few moments, and we went on our way.

Shortly after came news that Chief Seattle's grave had been vandalized. The headstone had been pushed off its pedestal and broken, and newspaper clippings about the housing project were left strewn around the gravesite.

I waited in vain for a religious or human rights leader to speak up so that I could join in offering condolences to the tribe. There were quotes from tribal leaders in the local papers conveying their shock and hurt, but silence from the nontribal community. Finally, I contacted the few people I knew in Suquamish and some friends from nearby Bainbridge Island, and I got back in touch with Ted George, who introduced me to other tribal elders. We called a meeting, and dozens of people attended who were likewise appalled at the desecration and the hostility. George and I became cochairs of a new group that formed that day in 2001, Suquamish Olalla Neighbors.

Over the course of several years, with the guidance of George and other tribal leaders, we educated ourselves about the tribe's history, values, and culture. We know enough about all the troubles of the reservation, he'd say. What we need to do is lift up the people who are bringing the community together and strengthening the culture. So we organized potlucks to celebrate those people and shower them with praise.

When hostile and disparaging statements appeared in the local newspaper or were voiced at public meetings, we countered them with our own statements of respect for the tribe and their rights.

In the past, hostile white neighbors had claimed to represent the entire nontribal community, but by showing up in large numbers at public meetings and by contributing letters to the newspaper, we were able to counter the influence of the anti-Indian voices.

In 2002, when a member of the Tribal Council contacted us, we joined with him and mobilized hundreds of supporters, nearby and across the state, to press for the return to the tribe of Old Man House Park, the state park where Chief Seattle's longhouse once stood. The same group of opponents who had fought the housing project geared up in a big way to prevent the return.

The day the State Parks Commission made the decision is a day I'll never forget. After months of our organizing, packing meetings, writing letters, visiting the commissioners, and bussing in supporters to the hearing held 65 miles away, and then after hours of testimony on all sides, the commission voted unanimously to return the park to the tribe. The gym where the meeting was held erupted in drumming and singing, the elders stepping up to shake the hand of each commissioner, tears flowing freely. On the bus ride home, Leonard Forsman, who is now chairman of the tribe, thanked those who participated. "We have to do this work as Indians, because it's our duty," he told the riders. "You don't have to, but you did it anyway. For that we thank you."

This history is now preserved in the Suquamish Museum. And the community is now different.

Ten years later, the predictions that the tribe would mismanage the park or exclude white folks haven't come true. The park is better cared for than ever and open to all. Perhaps that is why, instead of increasing after the victory, the hostility has faded away. A couple of the more outspoken residents left town, but most others simply turned their activist attention in more productive directions—like caring for other neighborhood parks.

And the tribe continues to get stronger, recovering its culture and building an economy that supports its members. In 2009, the tribe opened its newly built longhouse, "The House of Awakened Culture," as a successor to Old Man House.

Many factors have shifted the culture of our small community. The tribe's growing wealth as a result of income from its casino and other enterprises has allowed it to offer employment and services to addicted and traumatized members. Young people go to college, the tribe has built its own schools, and it is buying back land on the reservation. Plus, the tribe has given nearly half a million dollars over the last five years to nontribal educational and charitable programs.

The tribe is restoring the traditions of its people, including participating in an annual canoe journey, in which canoe families from dozens of tribes journey on the salt waters of the Salish Sea and sometimes out into the Pacific Ocean to reach the shores of the host tribe. I have been honored to be one of the pullers (paddlers) on those journeys for the last four years.

Suquamish Olalla Neighbors helps the tribe host canoe families from other tribes; dozens of volunteers bring food, serve, and clean up after sitting down with visiting tribal members for a meal. Former tribal chairman Bennie Armstrong told me after one of those occasions how he impressed the other tribal leaders, bragging, "When we want to do something, we just talk to our nontribal neighbors. We don't have to get out our lawyers or nothing!"

Are we going to lose it all?

In my community work, I could see real progress. We seemed to be resolving some important issues and learning to get along. And I'd hear the same thing from other place-based activists I talked to while researching articles for *YES! Magazine*. Locally, they got stuff done.

But at the larger scale, things seemed to be unraveling at a faster and faster pace. Extraordinary wildfires occur now every year. The ocean is acidifying, and just in the last year or so, all the starfish have disappeared from our beaches here in the Pacific Northwest, and scientists don't know why. Other species around the world are vanishing. Ecological systems are stressed, and many are dying.

People's lives are coming unraveled as well. Millions lost their homes as a result of predatory lending and Wall Street speculation. In Seattle, where a tech boom is pricing people out of the rental market, thousands of homeless people camp in parks and under bridges, and more low- and moderate-income people are displaced every day. People of color, who had the most tenuous foothold in the middle class, are especially hard hit. Inequality of wealth, mirrored by inequality in political power, is undermining the foundations of our democracy. Endless warfare seems to be baked into life now, shattering the lives of thousands of veterans and millions of refugees.

I believed when I helped found *YES!* that we humans are capable of so much more, and over the years, we have uncovered a lot of evidence that this is so. Nonetheless, the big trends are deeply disturbing.

Maybe I was wrong when I thought that we could avert collapse or dystopia. Maybe the momentum and power of the extractive economy is simply too strong, and, in spite of millions who want something different, maybe the big money, the military-industrial complex, the prison-industrial complex, and the frackers and drillers will win. That seemed to be happening.

Where would the universe send you?

I was agonizing over these issues when I stepped into Akaya Windwood's Oakland, California, office during a visit to the Bay Area.

Akaya is someone who quickly cuts through the small

talk. As head of the Rockwood Leadership Institute, a national training program for activists, she works with people who care deeply about the world and who devote their lives to making change. She knows that many of those people pay a personal price for their work, and that their own well-being and the effectiveness of their work are intertwined. So when she asked me how I was doing, it was not a casual question.

I'm worried, I told her.

Did we miss our chance to stop climate change and to heed Reverend Martin Luther King Jr.'s warning about the triple evils of racism, extreme materialism, and militarism?[2] And am I even looking in the right places for answers?

Akaya wasn't about to answer these questions. Instead, she asked another question. "If the universe could deploy the one small person that is you, what would it have you do?"

What I said next surprised me as much as it surprised her. "I'd go out traveling and see for myself."

I had not been thinking about a journey. But suddenly I knew that it was time for me to take a fresh look. It was time to go out and see for myself what was happening in our struggling communities. And I wanted to see if place-based work might hold clues to our future.

To find out, I would visit people at the margins of society who are the least embedded in the big institutions—big money, big corporations, big government—that reward status quo thinking. If the status quo is failing, I wanted to learn from those who have never been invited in, and those who have chosen to stay out.

I would avoid the power centers on the two coasts, and the progressive enclaves. I wanted to disrupt my comfort zone, meet new people, visit places I don't usually go, and learn what people care about and what they are doing about it.

"Once you say something like this, you can't un-say it," Akaya warned. When I left her office that day, I knew I was on my way.

Three questions

After talking with Akaya, I returned to Suquamish, and with a loan from the local credit union, I bought a small 2004 pickup truck and a tiny camper to fit in the truck bed. I negotiated time away from *YES!* and proposed to Steve Piersanti at Berrett-Kochler Publishers that I tell the story of my trip in a book. With the help of *YES!* colleagues, I started a blog site. Then I packed up my camper with food and bedding, clothes for the heat of a Great Plains summer and for a frigid Northeast winter, gifts to give away as I traveled, and a collection of books-on-tape for the long miles ahead.

As I prepared for my travels, I honed the questions I would be asking on my trip, and I narrowed them to these three.

1. **Is anti-racism work best done in communities?**
   At a time when Black Lives Matter was on the rise, and police were killing black people with impunity, could place-based work counter racism? In fact, is doing anti-racism work in person, in place, the only way to go deep enough to make it genuinely transformational? Were other people doing work like we did in Suquamish to combine justice and healing, and did it work?

2. **Climate change: Is local activism the way to both stop the extraction and transition to a sustainable future?**
   Before I left Seattle, I met with some of the kayakers who had earlier blockaded Shell Oil Company's huge drilling rig. The delays only lasted a few hours, but Shell did

eventually give up on drilling in the Arctic, and the
Obama administration canceled future drilling leases.
Likewise, the Keystone Pipeline encountered fierce
opposition both nationally and in the particular places
where the pipeline would run. I wondered, could we take
a stand against fossil fuels and rebuild most effectively
one community at a time?

3. **Can we build a new economy, rooted in our communities,**
   that can support us and protect the natural world?
   We need ways of meeting needs and providing livelihoods
   that don't extract wealth from most of the people of the
   world and from nature. Are communities succeeding
   in building locally rooted economies that offer real
   opportunities to all? If so, are they doing it without
   wrecking local ecosystems?

Fundamental to all of these questions is the one that comes
back to why it all matters. Do these innovations enliven people,
tapping into the creativity each of us has to offer, and do they,
likewise, revitalize the natural world?

A snail on wheels

Before I left to see what I could learn about these questions, I
did one more thing. I wanted to carry with me something that
would remind me of where I was starting from and where I
would return to. So I asked a young artist and Suquamish tribal
member, Kate Ahvakana, if she would paint an image on my
camper.

I thought she would do a small painting on the front of the
camper where it extends over the cab. But she and her boy-
friend, Toma Villa, who is also an artist, had a more ambitious

Kate Ahvakana, Suquamish tribal member,
with the images she painted on the front of the camper.

truck plan. Using spray paint, they turned the sides of the camper into a giant snail shell. Then they used ferns and cedar as stencils to paint patterns from the Pacific Northwest on the back. And on the front, Kate painted an emblem of Mother Earth, with two canoe heads, painted in Coastal Salish style, to represent a journey, and two paddles.

"The paddles face up to symbolize that you are traveling in peace and coming together with others to celebrate," Kate told me. "And the crescents and moons are to help you find the way back home."

I named the truck Caracol ("snail shell" in Spanish), because I would be carrying my home on my back. The snail also represented slow journalism; I would slow down enough to be with people and hear their story on their terms, and let them tell me what was important to them.

Caracol is also the term the Zapatistas use to designate the autonomous villages that are creating their own governance and their own ways of life. Caracol, with Kate and Toma's art, reminded me of Suquamish, of home, of the wisdom of indigenous peoples, and of the potential for those of us who are nonindigenous to also learn ways of life characterized by respect and reciprocity.

What I found

I started my journey in Montana and North Dakota, where I met Native women and men and ranchers who have stopped coal mining and fracking—and who are developing a vision for their region that can work for them and for future generations of ranchers and Native people. In Chicago, Detroit, Cincinnati, and other Rust Belt cities, I talked to urban farmers, worker-owners in the growing cooperative movement, and organizers building a new economy to take the place of the corporate economy that has failed these regions. In Greensboro, North Carolina, Harrisonburg, Virginia, and Ithaca, New York, I met people who are taking on their community's legacy of racism, and I traveled to Kentucky, where people are striving to restore Appalachian culture and to create a post-coal and post-racist future.

I met people working with the new activist mayor of Newark, New Jersey, and then traveled south and spent time with Christian leaders in Dallas, Texas, who believe that scripture tells them that all peoples, including Muslim immigrants, deserve to be welcomed. In a small Native pueblo north of Santa Fe, New Mexico, I met a young Navajo mother and midwife who is working to bring traditional birthing practices back to the community and to restore the health of the women who are in the best position to pass along well-being to the next generation.

The stories I found suggest that people are building power through place-based resistance and creativity, and as they do that, the outlines of a different society begin to emerge—one that is inclusive and healing; one that nourishes the soul and restores the landscape; one in which economies serve families and communities rather than the other way around.

Increasingly, people are seeing that these issues are not separable. Our health and well-being depend on the well-being of others, including nonhuman life. Reweaving relationships in the places we live provides a foundation for building a better world, and it gives people power that many didn't realize they had.

The people whose strategies were most powerful—that energized people and resulted in real change—do some combination of the following:

They build bridges among people who have been separated.
This work enables them to share power—especially across barriers of race and generation. They lift up the stories of those who have been silenced, and they reallocate power and wealth to those who have been excluded. They challenge systems that exclude and exploit. Done well, this effort builds trust and opens channels of connection that have long been blocked, unleashing unexpected joy and empowerment.

They reconnect to their ecological home.
For people in resource-rich areas, that may mean reclaiming the right to prevent their water, air, mountains, or soil from being sacrificed for the profit of extraction industries. In cities, it may mean urban farming, or protecting public use of green spaces and waterfronts. In any area, it means learning to deeply

understand the complex ecological systems we live within, so we can know how to protect and restore them while enhancing our well-being.

They rebuild the economy.
By building on local strengths and connecting to local needs, instead of using taxpayer subsidies to lure big corporations, they create livelihoods and a cycle of prosperity. These locally rooted economies avoid boom-and-bust cycles, reduce inequality, and restore dignity to work and entrepreneurship.

They take power.
They don't ask for permission, they just make stuff happen. They get involved in elections and government, but they set the agenda, rather than simply picking between column A and B, and they especially support the leadership of those who have been excluded. Locally based collaboration helps people break out of their isolation and experience their power.

Mural in Newark, New Jersey.

They carve out spaces for healing, creativity, and spirit. We come from many places in our communities, and trauma is one of them. Racism is a source of trauma that carries across generations, as are combat duty, sexual assault, and child abuse. Inclusive communities acknowledge the pain and offer safe spaces for refuge and healing. And they make space for celebration, beauty, and creativity, including spaces where art can tell the stories of the community.

Those who are most effective distance themselves from the consumptive mindset that is part of corporate media—many have consciously set out to decolonize their ways of life and their ways of thinking. They recognize that *we the people* are sovereign, and we have the right to create a better world.

We the people call this place our home

On a newly painted mural in one of the blighted neighborhoods I visited in Newark, New Jersey, is the phrase "We the People LOVE This Place." Out of the connection each of us have to place—our physical and ecological place and also our human community—we are creating profound change.

"In fact, we the people call this place our home," the mural continues. "We the people": an assertion of our power and our right to create in our own communities a way of life that works for all of us. "This place": an acknowledgment that whether we live in an urban neighborhood, a struggling small town, a suburb, or on a reservation, our place is our home.

Love: We evolved in family and community, in a place, and our connections make us who we are and give us power. By reclaiming that power, and by joining across barriers of race and ethnicity, ordinary people are making change happen.

Suquamish

Turtle Mountain
Reservation

Billings

Lame Deer

Fort Berthold

1. Setting Out, from

the North/Northwest

Fire, Coal, and Climate in Montana

It was the height of wildfire season in the West as I took off, a record-breaking year, and the air got smoky as I reached Montana.

A few days into my trip, I woke up at a campground south of Missoula to find a thin layer of black-and-white ash covering my truck and camper and the nearby pine trees. Driving in search of breakfast, I heard on the radio of the death of several firefighters in north-central Washington.

The smell of burning trees had followed me across Washington, Idaho, and into Montana along with the haze and the sting in the eyes and throat. An older couple I met at a coffee shop that morning told me that fires are common, but this fire season started earlier and was more intense than any they could remember.

A storm may be coming through in a few days, a young clerk at a run-down gas station and convenience store told me. Business was slow, and he had time to talk. It could bring winds that would blow the smoke away, he said. But it could also bring lightning strikes and set more fires in these bone-dry pine forests.

We risk passing tipping points where climate change takes on a life of its own, and it will be too late for humans to dial it back. We may have already passed some of these tipping points.

When more forests burn as a result of shifting climate patterns, and the burning releases more carbon, causing additional warming, we see this vicious cycle in action. Likewise, when receding ice cover in the Arctic leaves behind darker ocean waters, those waters absorb, rather than reflect, heat. Scientists have identified more than a dozen of these so-called positive feedback loops.

I thought about the salt waters where I live in Suquamish becoming acidic from the excess carbon, and the sea life that is dying. Then high in the Rockies as I crossed the Continental Divide, I saw evidence of the glaciers shrinking, year by year. For parts of the world that rely on runoff from mountain snowpacks, this is dire. I felt like I was witnessing a planet shift in real time. Instead of climate change being an abstraction of graphs and charts, I was seeing it in the changing waters, breathing it in the smoky air.

Journalists, scientists, policy makers, teachers, and other professionals are supposed to be dispassionate. We are trained to push aside our grief in favor of analysis and unbiased observation. Such practice is useful. But when we stand by as life on our beautiful planet dies, as one miraculous species after the next winks out, this stance turns from a professional calling into a pathology.

Cautiously, as I traveled, I let the lid off my grief.

Coal, from the Otter Creek Valley to China, and what happens in between

In Montana, I was looking for reasons to believe we can turn things around before we hit a climate Armageddon. I started with the people who were resisting plans for a giant new coal mine.

I first learned about the plans for the Otter Creek mine when controversy erupted about the transport of coal from the Powder River Basin in Montana and Wyoming to a proposed new coal export terminal in the Pacific Northwest.

The Gateway Pacific coal export terminal would be the largest in North America. It would be located some 100 miles north of Seattle on the traditional land of the Lummi Tribe. The terminal was designed to handle 54 million metric tons per year, most of which would be coal, according to the Washington State Department of Ecology.[1] Mile-and-a-half-long trains and giant ships, many from Asia, would cross waters and lands considered sacred by the Lummi people. SSA Marine, half owned by Goldman Sachs, was pushing the project.

The Lummi Tribe opposed the terminal. If any doubts existed about the strength of their opposition, they were laid to rest in September 2012, when tribal leaders stood on the beach of their homeland and set fire to a large facsimile of a check from port developers they stamped "non-negotiable."

Lummi tribal members, like most of those in Indian Country, are not wealthy. But the tribe made it clear that money would not buy their support for a project they believed would threaten the clean water needed to support their fisheries and the sanctity of their traditional lands. The tribe has treaty rights to fish in these waters, which gives it the legal standing to block the terminal.

Lummi tribal members aren't the only ones who would be affected by this massive new coal mine and port project. Large numbers of Bellingham residents also oppose the project, and they elected a slate of county commissioners who were outspoken opponents to the terminal. The coal would be cheap enough to make it attractive to Asian nations, such as China, where toxic pollution is causing 1.6 million premature deaths a year, according to research cited in *The Guardian*.[2] And it would add still more carbon to the atmosphere, worsening the climate crisis.

Then there are those who live adjacent to the source of this coal, the residents of the Otter Creek Valley in southeast Montana and the neighboring ranchers and members of the Northern Cheyenne Tribe. Arch Coal proposed to strip-mine this area, creating the largest such mine in Montana. The mine would yield 1.2 billion tons of coal over 20 years and be located in what is now a quiet valley of ranches and creeks near the boundaries of the Custer National Forest.

Arch Coal and its partners, including the Burlington Northern Railroad, would build an 86-mile railroad spur to get the coal to the main train line. The new rail line would follow the Tongue River, which borders the Northern Cheyenne Reservation, and cross ranches, many of which have been in the same family for generations.

"The only way the railroad spur can be built is to force it on the ranchers," Dawson Dunning told me when I sat down with him at a coffee shop in Livingston, Montana, just outside Yellowstone Park. Dunning, age 32, is a member of a family that has operated a ranch in the Otter Creek Valley since 1890. He has a round, open face, blue eyes, and a short beard. Instead of the stereotypical cowboy hat, he wore a baseball cap and shades, and he plans to return to that remote valley to operate the ranch

Dawson Dunning comes from a family of Otter Creek Valley ranchers.

when his father retires. To him, the Otter Creek Valley is home, and he doesn't want it destroyed.

Those ranchers and their organization, the Northern Plains Resource Council, along with the Northern Cheyenne Tribe, the National Wildlife Federation, and the Sierra Club, are at the core of the resistance to the mining project and railroad spur.

In support of this resistance, Lummi carver Jewell Praying Wolf James and his crew carved a totem pole and announced they would offer it as a gift to the Northern Cheyenne Tribe. I decided I would be there when it arrived on the reservation on August 30.

Another Way of Ranching

I stopped for the night in Billings, Montana, at an RV campground on the Yellowstone River. There was a breeze off the river, and with the camper vent opened, I could stay cool while I caught up on email and planned my next stops. Through the window of the camper, I could see a ridge rising straight from the river to a rocky peak above.

I'd heard that RV campgrounds were great places to meet other travelers, families and retired people who pulled up folding chairs around a campfire to swap stories and crisp marshmallows. Not true here. The giant RVs lined up along the pavement dwarfed my pickup truck camper. The park offered both WiFi and cable television, and the RVs were self-contained, with their own bathrooms and showers. On the pebbly banks of the Yellowstone River, I had the rushing water and the sunrise to myself.

I had stopped in Billings to meet the ranchers who have been fighting coal in Montana since the 1970s. I met Steve Charter, chairman of the Northern Plains Resource Council, at the organization's headquarters, and he invited me to

Steve Charter is chairman of the Northern Plains Resource Council and owns a ranch north of Billings, Montana.

walk out on his land to the north and to park my truck there for the night.

Charter wore a cowboy hat, a green cotton shirt, jeans held up by a belt with a silver buckle, and scruffy boots. His neatly trimmed beard showed some white amid the black.

He was just a teenager when his parents gathered with neighbors to found a landowners association to fight coal, he told me. "In the early 1970s, these land men from big eastern coal companies started showing up at our doors. They were pretty heavy-handed: 'We're coming in, and we'll offer you a reasonable price, and you'll sell to us.' And then they would say, 'Your neighbors have all made deals.'"

The Charter family, who lived in the remote Bull Mountains about 50 miles north of Billings, called their neighbors and learned that, in fact, they hadn't cut deals with the coal company. They met and formed the Bull Mountain Landowners Association.

"The coal companies didn't like that," Charter recalled with a chuckle. "Coming from Appalachia, they were used to strong-arming people and getting their way."

Like many stories of the West, the railroad has a role here. The federal government had granted railroad companies vast tracts of land in exchange for building the rail lines and serving the farmers, ranchers, and rural towns. But, according to Charter, the rail companies prefer large trains that carry single commodities, like coal. They dropped passenger services to small towns and shipments of cattle, farm products, and other local goods. Their preference for coal, together with their ownership of alternating square-mile blocks of land, made them a formidable foe.

"We weren't in a strong position to fight," Charter said. "If we lost the [grazing] leases, we'd just end up with a checkerboard of unusable land, so the coal companies had a good argument about why we should cave in and sell out to them."

But they didn't sell out.

"We loved the land and didn't want it torn up," Charter explained. "Also, my dad was an ornery rancher and didn't like being threatened and pushed around."

They soon learned that other groups of landowners were also forming associations, including the ranchers at Otter Creek. So the groups from around the state met up in the Charters' living room and formed the Northern Plains Resource Council.

This wasn't long after the first Earth Day, in April 1970, and environmental consciousness was spreading. Young people just out of college heard about these ranchers who were battling coal, and they began to show up and volunteer. Those young people, and Steve Charter, who was just out of high school, became the first volunteer staff.

At first, the ranchers were leery of the newcomers, Charter told me. Many of the young people had long hair, which didn't go over well in conservative eastern Montana. "There were a lot of haircuts," Charter recollected.

But somehow it worked out. "As people worked together and got to know each other, that's when the magic happened."

At Montana's 1972 legislative session, a coalition of ranchers, hippies, and environmentalists pushed through some of the country's most progressive environmental regulations, including laws requiring coal companies to restore the land after they mined it. They reached out to Appalachian anti-coal groups and the people there who had been "exploited and messed with for years," as Charter put it. In conjunction with the Appalachian groups, the council lobbied for a national mine reclamation act,[1] which, after years of work, was adopted by Congress and signed into law by President Jimmy Carter on August 3, 1977.

Although they had help from some of the big green groups, Charter said the local groups from Appalachia and Montana led the work, and that, he believed, made the difference. "We're Ground Zero," Charter told me. "We know the issues because we live them. That gives us credibility."

Today, Charter is painfully aware that the issue of coal affects far more than the people who live adjacent to mines and train tracks. "Every ton of coal they mine can be translated into carbon dioxide. So we're all Ground Zero," Charter stated. "It's a nineteenth-century fuel, and this is the twenty-first century. All of the time and effort trying to prop up the coal industry would be better spent trying to figure out an alternative economy that's going to work in the long run."

The conversation then took a tack I wasn't expecting. It turned out that Charter had some interesting ideas about how to jump-start that economy. We were walking on the rocky, dry ground of his ranch, where a small rise allowed an expansive view of grasslands, prickly cactus, more outcroppings, and, off in the distance, the highway back to Billings.

Charter explained that since 1984 he had been practicing "holistic resource management," a technique for herding cattle that mimics the behavior of wild ungulates, like buffalo, when predators are nearby. In this case, ranchers use fencing to keep the cattle together, so their hooves grind up the grassland and they defecate and urinate on the ground, spread seeds, and then get moved off it. Although there is some controversy over when and where this method works, research indicates that land managed this way is healthier than when cattle are dispersed over a large area and plant life doesn't fully recover between grazings.[2] The U.S. Department of Agriculture is among those institutions endorsing the technique. The system works best when the person managing the land understands it well and can observe the health of the land year by year to learn what amount of grazing and recovery time is optimal.

Charter only recently began to see an additional dimension to restorative grazing—its connection to climate change. Overgrazing, tilling, and other modern farming practices have depleted the carbon in the soil, allowing it to escape into the atmosphere. But restoring the soil contributes to the soil's ecological diversity and health and to the productivity of the grasslands. And it also helps the soil absorb massive amounts of carbon. Mycorrhizal fungi accomplishes some of this magic. It extends fine filaments far into the ground, releasing enzymes, dissolving rocks, and bringing nutrients up to the surface.

Microbes become part of complex food chains and carbon chains, Charter explained, and eventually form the humus that extends deep into the soil. That humus is basically made up of carbon. So ranchers could manage their land to dramatically increase the soil's absorption of carbon, making rangeland a giant sponge for excess carbon dioxide. This type of soil also holds rainwater more effectively, preventing runoff and flooding downstream and reducing the need for irrigation. The soil's capacity to hold water will become a critical issue as the climate continues to change and rainfall becomes more erratic, threatening vast areas with desertification.

"It's really exciting. There's a whole movement of people who are figuring out how to build soil in ways nobody had thought about. And people are getting amazing results," Charter said. Restorative grazing could allow ranchers to increase the productivity of rangeland "without having to give all the money to Monsanto" for fertilizers. "You're getting your prosperity from the soil, and you're building it over time," he said.

This form of ranching could add up to an agrarian renaissance of sorts, if Charter is correct, because it would require more workers. And this could help reverse the depopulation of rural America.

"They almost brag that we're down to half a percent of the population making their living from agriculture," he said. "There is no relationship to the land anymore. There's just someone driving a huge tractor, putting on all these chemicals." And when few people are needed to work the land, the small towns shrink.

"So this could totally turn that around. It's going to require a lot of knowledge, a lot of hands-on working with the land, because intensively managing livestock takes knowledge and it takes labor. But that's a good thing. This is the kind of job that people like doing once they know how to do it. As ranchers, we hope to bring people back to where human knowledge and hands will do this, and not petrochemicals and running tractors."

I looked around at the dry land, covered in grasses and cactus, the hills, and the dusk that was beginning to settle. In the distance, headlights moved up and down the highway to Billings. As an outsider, I had assumed this land was how it always would be. But I could see that if it gets a bit drier, it could become desert. My later research showed that nearly 30 million acres are lost to desertification each year,[3] a rate that is 30 times or more the historic rate of land loss.

But Charter envisions a day when the soil is returned to health, with complex ecosystems of microbes and fungi in symbiotic relationships that stabilize the soil, build its structure, and absorb and hold rainwater. The soil would also steadily soak up carbon from the atmosphere, storing it safely in the humus, reversing climate change.

And young people once again would work the land; there would be jobs for people with the patience and work ethic to deeply know the land. And the economy and communities of rural America would recover.

That night, I slept well in my camper parked outside Charter's barn, my rest interrupted only by the yelps and whines of coyotes in the distance and a glimpse of the star-filled sky.

In the morning, I stopped in to say good-bye. Inside his passively heated solar house, partially dug into the bank to keep it insulated from Montana's frigid winters, Charter and his partner were making breakfast. While she made a veggie smoothie, he was working up some bacon, eggs, and coffee before taking off to check on his cattle.

The Ranchers and Native People Resisting the Otter Creek Mine

I drove southeast from Billings, my truck slowing as I climbed the long, grassy hills and then catching up to traffic on the downslope side. I was headed toward the North ern Cheyenne Reservation. Alaina Buffalo Spirit, one of the opponents of the mine, had invited me to camp on her land and to meet her friends and extended family, and then to go together to attend the welcoming ceremony when the Lummi carvers arrived with their totem pole. When I asked her what I could bring, she suggested fruits and vegetables, which are hard to come by on the reservation.

The land in this part of Montana is open and sparsely populated. Lame Deer is home to both tribal headquarters and Chief Dull Knife Community College. I passed through the town and continued several miles to reach Buffalo Spirit's home, a brand-new but modest house, with a brightly painted teepee in the front yard and fields in all directions. Beyond the fields lay a couple of other houses, and then hillsides covered in stands of pines interspersed with grasslands.

It was blazing hot and dry when I arrived, and there was no shade. I was grateful to enter the darkened, air-conditioned home and for ice water as I listened to her story.

Alaina Buffalo Spirit: I spoke up for you

Buffalo Spirit has long, wispy, brown hair and a ready smile. She showed me a few of her paintings—one of women on horseback who, she says, wore their finest to battle, knowing it might be their last day.

Buffalo Spirit grew up living with her parents and grandparents in a one-room log cabin and speaking the Northern Cheyenne language. "My grandfather was a farmer along the Tongue River," she told me. "And he was a leader in the Sundance ceremony. My grandfather could heal people."

Buffalo Spirit had six brothers and two sisters, and the family was poor but didn't lack for food. "We learned about the edible plants along the river, like rosehips and milkweed, the wild mint tea—you can smell it as you walk along the river. We made homemade fishing poles with safety pins, and we'd catch catfish, bring it home, and fry it. And there was deer, venison; my grandmother and mother would hang it outside to dry. We pretty much lived off the land."

Their home was surrounded by ponderosa pine trees. "It's not desolate and desert like everyone might think; there are a lot of grasses and natural sage and plants we use for ceremonies."

Buffalo Spirit remembers happy times with her family, although she also remembers the challenges of living in a one-room cabin, where they used a hand pump to draw water from the well for the home and garden.

"My grandfather had a team of horses. We would jump on the wagon with him and my grandmother, my mom, aunties,

Alaina Buffalo Spirit by the Tongue River on her family's land.
The proposed train line would run along the opposite side of the river.

and cousins, and go pick wild plums. They had a portable stove, and my grandma would cook up the soup, and she used to have homemade biscuits and coffee. As children, we never had candy. So our dessert was to have a bowl of coffee, sweetened, and dip the biscuits in it. And we'd eat all the plums we could."

Later, she took me down to her family's land at the edge of the clear, fast-running Tongue River. The quiet there was striking—the only sounds were the river running by and the wind through the cottonwood trees. The heat of the long summer day baked the ground, but in the shade it was breezy and green.

"My grandmother shared with me that this water is sacred," she said. "That's why I believe we need to protect our river." The family still conducts ceremonies there, she told me. "The proposed railroad would run just a few feet from this river, just right over there on the other side. It would disturb this quiet valley and pollute it. I don't want to see that."

The hills above the Tongue River and the Otter Creek Valley are filled with places of spiritual significance to members of the Northern Cheyenne Tribe. Many of their ancestors are buried nearby, and the thought of their gravesites being dynamited to open the mine or to make way for the railroad spur is an anathema.

Buffalo Spirit, like most members of the Northern Cheyenne Tribe, opposes construction of the railroad and mine. She worries about the huge influx of people who would arrive to work at the mine. Many in this region have heard stories of the crime, violence, and abuse of women and children that came to towns in North Dakota along with the Bakken oil boom. "I can go down to camp by the river, and no one disturbs me," she told me. "And I would like that for my grandkids and for their kids as well." Plus, as a cancer survivor, she doesn't want to be exposed to coal dust, diesel, and other pollutants.

"I'm a grandmother, and I'm going to be a great-grandma soon. What would I tell my grandkids if they said, 'Grandma, what did you do to stop this? What did you do to help save our water and our land and our air?' They might ask me that, and I'll be able to say, 'Here are the records and the articles. Here—I spoke up for you.'"

That night Buffalo Spirit's extended family came by, and the women bustled in the kitchen preparing a meal as the men told stories and jokes. The conversation went on well into the night, around the fire pit next to the teepee, with the sparks flying up to join the bright Montana stars.

The ceremony to welcome the totem pole

I woke up in the morning to the sound of thunder and wind, and the camper shuddering in the gusts. Dark marbled clouds covered the sky, and a warm breeze followed a brief but brilliant sunrise. Buffalo Spirit and other visitors who had come to witness the ceremony were still asleep in the house and the teepee.

Later, we piled into cars and drove to the site where the ceremony was to take place. The totem pole was already there, lashed to the back of a yellow flatbed truck. Smoke from distant forest fires had turned the intense late August sunlight gray-blue. The wind blew steadily, rustling the cottonwood trees and sage. In all directions were rocky hillsides and buttes, with the river cutting its way among the outcroppings and greening the shrubs along the banks. The area has been used by tribes going back 10,000 years, the tribe's archaeologists told the crowd.

The crowd was a mix of people from the Northern Cheyenne Tribe and nearby ranches, a smattering of environmentalists from Billings and elsewhere, and visitors from the Lummi Tribe.

The bluffs across the river would be dynamited to create the right grade for the new railroad spur, rancher Hank Coffin told me as we waited for the ceremony to begin. He and his wife, Kitty Coffin, a member of the Northern Cheyenne Tribe, would see their land broken into two parts if the rail construction went through.

"It is strange to think that a railroad would want to knock that high hill down so they could go right through the middle of it, but that's what they're after," he said. The Coffins, like the other ranch and tribal families here, aren't giving in. "We are *we the people* of the great state of Montana."

On this day, there was still time to stop the dynamite, the giant excavating machines, the strip mining, and the new coal trains. That fact added a seriousness of purpose to the scene. On this day, instead of dynamite explosions, there were only the sounds of the wind, the children playing, and the adults hauling in food for a shared meal and setting up chairs in rows facing tables for the speakers.

The ceremony began with a prayer and continued with speeches, songs, and more prayers. The carver of the pole, Jewell Praying Wolf James, along with Freddy Lane and others from the Lummi Tribe, talked about the pole they had carved and then transported from their home near Bellingham, Washington. As they made their way to the Northern Cheyenne Reservation, they visited various communities, churches, reservations, and a synagogue to explain the battle to stop the Gateway Pacific coal terminal in Washington State and the Otter Creek mine in Montana. All spoke of their determination to protect the human and natural communities that make their homes in these threatened places.

"We're standing on sacred ground," one of the ranchers, Roger Sprague, told me during a break in the ceremony.

Jewell Praying Wolf James from the House of Tears carving studio, with the totem pole he and his team carved.

Sprague is tall, heavy-set but fit, and sported a broad-rimmed cowboy hat and a bushy, graying mustache. His family came to this valley in 1881, he said, and they raised cattle and traded with the Cheyenne people. Sprague has spent his whole life in this valley, and one of his two sons works with him on the ranch. Sprague told me he hopes his grandchildren will take over the ranch someday.

"When I ride horseback through this country, we find arrowheads, teepee rings, places where indigenous people lived. We respect that, and we want to protect it. Just like my family history, we want to protect that, too."

James and his team of carvers consulted with members of the Northern Cheyenne before carving the pole, to ensure they included appropriate symbols. The pole contains badgers, who protect the ground; an iconic buffalo; and an eagle clutching a rabbit, which represents the processes of the ecosystems, Jewell explained. And the Cheyenne medicine wheel has a blue outer circle to represent the water of life.

"Part of our prayer and our belief is that water is the blood of Mother Earth," Jewell James said when we spoke after the ceremony. "We don't have the right to destroy her. If we don't stand up and unite, we may find out we're just a cancer that killed her."

Fighting extraction

The people gathered on this knoll came from very different backgrounds, but they had much more in common than their opposition to a mine and a railroad addition. They are each, in their own way, rejecting the ethos of extraction.

"We're a commodity colony," Alexis Bonogofsky told me. Bonogofsky, who has been working on coal issues for many years, is from a ranching family in southeast Montana and also is on the staff of the National Wildlife Federation. "We're told all we're worth is under our feet."

"This coal is to make big corporations a lot of money," Sprague told me. "And they'll do it on the backs of us small ranchers."

"We already have global warming, and the ocean and the rivers are warming up," Jewell James said. "We're all in the same battle; we're all looking at a holocaust if we don't stand up."

James takes some solace in the idea that prominent non-Natives are speaking up for the environment. "The pope said, 'God did give you dominion over the Earth, but you're also to respect it because it's God's creation. Keep it holy. Everything on the Earth is your brother and sister.' In the 400 to 500 years of contact, that's what we always hoped would finally be understood on the other side."

That shift, from an economy of extraction to one of reciprocity with the Earth and with one another, is foundational.

The ranchers recognize that the Native people lived in this region many generations before their families. Still, they share with their Northern Cheyenne neighbors the responsibility that goes with inheriting the area from their ancestors, and the duty to pass it along in good condition to their descendants. That responsibility has meant a struggle against extraction industries that has gone on for years. The ranchers' and the Northern Cheyenne's shared attachment to their place, and to the human and natural communities that comprise it, is a source of real power.

"People care about this land and have an attachment to it and will put up a fight," Brad Sauer said. Sauer ranches north of the ceremonial site, near where the Colstrip mines were located. "We'll stay up late at night to read documents and write letters, and go places to testify. It all starts with a deep attachment to the land."

At the end of the ceremony, members of both tribes—one coastal, one plains—ranchers, and activists from the Sierra Club and the National Wildlife Federation circled around, each shaking the hands of the speakers, carvers, visitors, and singers. Then the food was brought out, people chatted and sang and drummed, and the restless children were finally allowed to play on the totem pole.

Otter Creek Valley

On my last day in Montana, I drove to Otter Creek to see the valley that would become a strip mine if Arch Coal has its way.

The Otter Creek Valley is made up of ranches and open fields, forest stands, and a creek nestled between the rocky outcroppings and ponderosa pines of the Custer National Forest. I pulled over by the side of the narrow road that follows the creek up the valley. It was so quiet there that a footfall in the grass sounds loud, and you hear, not traffic or airplanes, but the rustle of birds in the dry brush and the rush of water. I tried to imagine the excavations, coal trains, and deep pit that would overtake this valley if Arch Coal's plans were approved.

This question matters beyond the Otter Creek Valley and the Tongue River, and beyond the Northern Cheyenne Reservation and the ranches that border it. The implications extend beyond the towns and valleys bisected by the rail lines, and the giant new coal terminal that could be forced on the Lummi Tribe, and even beyond Beijing, Tianjin, Shanghai, and other Chinese cities where millions are sickened by breathing coal-polluted air.

If scientists are correct that more than three quarters of

the carbon now in the ground needs to stay there to avert cata-
strophic climate disruption, then the fate of this coal is not just
the problem of those millions. It's a problem for all of human-
ity—and for almost all other species.

For every ton of coal burned, 2.86 tons of carbon dioxide
are released into the atmosphere, according to the U.S. Energy Information Administration.[1] The Otter Creek mine alone
would produce 1.2 billion tons of coal. The coal from this one
project, not including the climate consequences of excavation
and transport, would contribute more than 3 billion tons of
carbon dioxide to an already saturated atmosphere. That is the
equivalent of putting 600 million additional cars on the road
for a year.[2]

Here in southeast Montana, this small but powerful collaboration of Native people, ranchers, and environmentalists was
helping to avert not only a local disaster but a global one.

Postscript

As I was completing work on this book, Arch Coal announced
that it had withdrawn its application to mine for coal at Otter
Creek. The company cited low coal prices and uncertainty about
permits—uncertainty that was at least in part a result of the
activism of the tribes, the ranchers, and the environmentalists.

Not long after, the Army Corps of Engineers announced
that, in light of the Lummi Tribe's treaty fishing rights, it would
not grant a permit to build the Gateway Pacific terminal.

A North Dakota Reservation Where Fracking Rules

FORT BERTHOLD, NORTH DAKOTA—
The haze from the wildfires burning in Washington and Montana followed me as I left the Otter Creek Valley and headed northeast toward North Dakota. The land was open grasslands with few trees. The late August sun was unrelenting, temperatures climbing into the upper 90s. I reluctantly left the back roads for Interstate 94, hoping to finish the 400-mile drive to Fort Berthold before dark.

As the day progressed, the soot and smog from methane flares and, I assumed, fracking by-products deepened the haze and added an odor of hydrocarbons. The flares were my first signal that I was coming into Bakken oil country. Then well pumps began to appear in farm fields, like giant grasshoppers bowing again and again in front of bright orange methane flares. The flaring of natural gas is so widespread it can be seen at night from space, competing with the nation's major cities for brightness in satellite images.

This is boom country. The number of wells in use in North Dakota nearly quadrupled to more than 12,000 from 2004 to

2014;[1] oil extraction increased twelvefold; the state now pumps more than a million barrels a day and is contributing to the massive increase in domestic oil extraction of the last decade.

I headed to the Fort Berthold Reservation, where half of the 14,000 members of the three affiliated tribes of the Mandan, Hidatsa, and Arikara Nations make their home.[2] The MHA Nation is located at the heart of this fracking boom.

I had called Cedar Gillette before I began my trip to learn how this extraction boom was affecting the people she works with. Gillette is part Turtle Mountain Chippewa, but she is a member of the MHA Nation and had worked as a domestic violence advocate in Fort Berthold. She told me about the massive influx of oil workers with money to spend. The so-called "man camps"—the large, temporary housing sites where the drilling workers (and almost all of them are men) reside—were

View west over Lake Sakakawea, formed when the Missouri River was dammed. The haze from wildfires and gas flaring is visible in the distance.

creating unsafe conditions, both for local women and for the wives and girlfriends from out of town who accompanied the newcomers.

Sex trafficking and sexual assaults are widespread, according to Gillette. And drugs are abundant: heroin, methamphetamine, and others. Organized crime is rampant. "People are fearful," she told me.

And for good reason. Violent crime rates rose 121 percent from 2005 to 2011, according to FBI figures. "These dramatic increases have overwhelmed state, local, and tribal law enforcement agencies," according to the federal National Drug Control Strategy.[3]

The tribes' environmental oversight is likewise overwhelmed. Contaminated material, including radioactive byproducts of fracking, have been found dumped on the reservation. The MHA Nation lacks the resources to oversee the many drilling sites and waste facilities.

These costs, along with other expenses of the boom—from damaged roads to social services for the flood of new workers and their families—have eaten up the cash windfall that was supposed to support the tribes for years. Now, with oil prices in a slump, meeting those needs is even more out of reach, according to a report by the Property and Environmental Research Center.[4]

I got lost when I arrived in the pitch dark in Fort Berthold. I had called ahead to see about staying in the RV campground behind the tribal casino. No one is there after six, I was told. Just camp tonight and register in the morning.

The casino was easy to find, right on the main highway and well lit. But I drove around in the dark through construction yards and newly excavated dirt roads for a long time before I finally found the dozens of RVs parked way behind the casino.

The electrical outlet at my site didn't work, and the bathroom was nowhere to be found. I went to sleep that night uneasily, recalling stories of murder and kidnapping.

In the morning, I crossed the artificial lake created by the Garrison Dam on my way to New Town, North Dakota. The name New Town came about when the Native people living in the villages along the Missouri River were forced to relocate to make way for a dam that would flood their homes. After trying for many years to prevent the dam construction, they finally were left with no choice but to move. Someone stuck a sign in the ground at the place they would resettle; the sign read, "new town," I was told, and no one ever bothered to come up with a different name.

I had come to see Prairie Rose Seminole, a member of the Arikara Tribe, to learn about the impacts of fracking on the tribal community. But when we met at the Boys and Girls Club where she works, she wanted to talk about food, health, and healing.

Seminole is tall, thoughtful, and talkative. She wore a jeans jacket over a lacy white skirt. She grew up in Fargo, North Dakota, she told me, one of six kids. Her father had a huge garden, and he passed along his gardening skills to Prairie Rose and her sisters, in violation of the Arikara tradition, which calls on skills to be passed down to daughters from mothers, not fathers.

"We'd go out and forage and get stone fruits and berries and roots, turnips and stuff, and preserve those for the year. Some of the good memories I have of being a kid were foraging and fishing."

After she was diagnosed with a chronic disease, her interest in healthy food increased. Today she teaches young tribal members about how to find food and medicine in the wild.

*Prairie Rose Seminole at one of her favorite
foraging spots on the Fort Berthold Reservation.*

"We've always had a spiritual connection to the food, and to the earth that grows that food, and to the water that feeds that food, and to the air that the food grows into," she said. "There's a balance, and we fit into that as caretakers. I don't want to romanticize who we are, but we've gotten so far away from that."

She took me to one of her favorite foraging sites just outside of New Town and showed me where she gathers chokecherries, plums, and a variety of medicinal plants. But she worries that the food is contaminated by oil and gas emissions and fracking chemicals. She had the soil at one site tested, and it came up clean for the listed contaminants. Still, she has questions.

"Oil development has jeopardized our sacred sources of food," she said. "If the water is contaminated, no one is telling the chokecherry bush not to drink that water, no one is telling the deer not to eat those chokecherries. You have no idea if you're eating a deer that's contaminated.

"We're a population that deals with a high number of chronic illnesses that could be prevented through our diet. If our traditional diet and food systems are contaminated, then we're not doing ourselves any good.

"We're losing our foods and medicines because of the oil impact, and that's a huge cultural loss—that's just as devastating to me as losing language."

Food is only one reason Prairie Rose regrets the oil and gas boom.

Drugs and crime have taken their toll; the millions of dollars that have flooded the community have made some tribal members extremely wealthy, while most continue to struggle. Elected members of the tribal council are swayed by big payoffs, she believes. And she sees little evidence that the cash that flowed through the tribe is compensating for the crime, overcrowding, and pollution. Nor does she think it is developing the long-term economic foundation that could sustain them now as the boom ends.

"When you drive through Turtle Mountain, it's beautiful, green lands—they're now the medicine chest of the Dakotas, where we once were," she said wistfully.

The Turtle Mountain Reservation, where fracking is banned, was to be my next stop.

No Fracking Way Turtle Mountain

TURTLE MOUNTAIN RESERVATION, NORTH DAKOTA—Drive the long, straight roads of north-central North Dakota, and you pass lake after lake, amid hay fields and forests. Migratory birds, attracted by the abundance of water and grain, pause here. Farmers, boaters, and fishermen orient their lives around the pure water.

The water, more than anything, explains why members of the Turtle Mountain Band of Chippewa Indians acted so quickly when they learned their region was next in line for fracking. Within just a few weeks of the tribal women's meeting on the topic in late 2011, the council banned fracking on the 77,000-acre reservation. Their ban was among the first in North America, and it has since been upheld by succeeding tribal councils.

The process started in November 2011 when an elder, Carol Davis, called the women of the Turtle Mountain Tribe together. Fracking was booming on the Fort Berthold Reservation just a couple hundred miles away, and Davis had heard that the Turtle Mountain Reservation could be next. In the tribe's tradition,

53

women are responsible for protecting the water, so she invited the women to discuss fracking over a meal.

"I didn't want to go," Christa Monette told me when I met her at a restaurant in the tribe's Sky Dancer Casino, where she works in the gift shop. "But then my sister said, 'They're having supper!' And I was like, 'Oh, I suppose.'"

When she first heard about fracking in Fort Berthold, Monette thought an oil and gas boom on her remote reservation would be a good thing. "I remember thinking, 'Wow, how lucky they are! How come we can't strike oil here?'" But after Davis explained her concerns to the group of women, Monette and her half-sister, Cedar Gillette, decided they needed to learn more about the process of hydraulic fracturing, or fracking.

At a second meeting, Davis offered each of the women a tobacco leaf, telling them to accept it only if they were committed to work on the issue. Monette took the tobacco reluctantly: She was a single mother of three, working full time. But the more the women—and the men who joined them—learned about fracking, the more worried they became.

They learned how the process works—that large amounts of water mixed with chemicals, salts, and sand are forced deep into the ground to shatter rock in order to release methane and oil. They learned that the procedure results in large volumes of wastewater and contaminated materials. And they learned that the drilling would go right through their precious aquifer, risking contamination of drinking water and lakes. If that happened, cleanup could be impossible. They also learned about Dimock, Pennsylvania, where a well explosion and contaminated groundwater were linked to fracking.

Another dimension makes this issue personal for Gillette and Monette. The half-sisters have parents on the two reservations, and each of them has spent time in both Fort Berthold and Turtle Mountain. "I didn't want both my homelands to be fracked," Gillette said.

Armed with this knowledge, Gillette, Monette, and others in the Turtle Mountain group brought their findings to the Turtle Mountain Tribal Council on November 2, 2011.

"People were stunned when we presented the facts," Gillette said.

The council called a second meeting and invited the entire community. At that meeting, the council unanimously voted to ban fracking.

"What is sacred to our tribe is water," tribal chairman Richard McCloud told me when I met him in his office on the Turtle Mountain Reservation. "We all know that in the very near future, water will be more valuable than oil or gold or anything else.

"This area is where our ancestors did their farming; the springs run through here, and this is how generations survived. The fracking ban will protect our water so future generations can continue to survive."

Still, for Gillette, the meeting was tense. "I didn't believe [the ban] would pass until they all said yes," she said. After all, the elected council of an impoverished tribe was voting to leave millions of dollars on the table.

What the sisters didn't know when the fracking ban passed was that the Bureau of Indian Affairs had been on the brink of opening Turtle Mountain land for oil and gas leasing. The tribe's action put a halt to the leasing.

Four years later, in early 2015, the tribal council adopted a new water code that solidifies the tribe's stance on fracking.

McCloud said he has no regrets when I asked him about the money the tribe could have received in drilling royalties.

"I'm a small-business owner. I make my money the old-fashioned way," he stated. "I earn it." McCloud said he tracks the

The Turtle Mountain Chippewa Tribe is turning to wind and solar instead of fracking. This windmill helps power the Turtle Mountain Community College.

news on the Fort Berthold Reservation. "Whoever said money buys happiness, I have yet to see that."

Before I left Turtle Mountain, I decided to follow Monette's advice and visit the reservation's community college. I wasn't sure why she had urged me to go there, but as soon as I turned off the highway and drove up the approach road, I understood. The college sits next to one of the many tree-lined lakes that dot the reservation. And standing tall above the college is a windmill. The windmill helps supply electricity to the college, but it also suggests what's possible. The area has been rated Class 5 for wind potential, and the tribe is working with support from the U.S. Department of Energy to develop the abundant wind— and solar—energy resources of the reservation.

Gillette is now attending law school with a focus on environmental law. Monette is still on the Turtle Mountain Reservation, still a busy working mom, except she's now the main administrator of the "No Fracking Way Turtle Mountain" Facebook page, where she posts not only about her reservation but also about others around the world resisting fossil fuel extraction.

A choice of futures

The resource-rich West faces a choice about the future: continue the extraction and expand the sacrifice zones, or take the route that Gillette, Monette, and many of the ranchers and Native people favor—phase out dependence on extractive mining and drilling industries, and convert to a sustainable, or even a restorative, economy.

The extraction industries will incur job losses. The coal industry is already in decline, and low oil prices have slowed the oil boom as well. There are only about 1,300 jobs in the coal industry in Montana, according to the U.S. Energy Information Administration.[1] The state's outdoor recreation industry, by contrast, employs 64,000.[2]

But there is potential for much more. A new, even larger workforce will be needed for the new economy. Restorative grazing and soil management, and renewable energy generation and conservation require larger numbers of skillful workers than do current practices. And the jobs created this way aren't the boom-and-bust sort that disrupt communities, create the conditions for crime, and then leave contaminated land and water in their wake.

This restorative economy will be of little use to transnational corporations and Wall Street banks because much of the profit will come in forms that can't be readily extracted from the region. Instead, the benefits will flow right back to the communities: Clean water for drinking and irrigation. Clean air. Fewer inducements for the unscrupulous to turn to corruption and crime. Livelihoods that are anchored on the land and a renaissance for rural communities. This approach contributes to solving the climate crisis. And it means healthier, longer lives, and enhanced quality of life for generations to come.

Plaque at Turtle Mountain Community College.

When people have a chance to study, discuss, and decide on options, they favor this sustainable path. A majority of Americans said they would be willing to pay more for electricity generated via renewables, for example, according to a *New York Times*/CBS poll.[3] Sixty percent favor developing alternatives to fossil fuel, according to the Pew Research Center.[4]

The extraction industries win many of their battles anyway, though, because they have so much money to throw at the political process—something most communities don't have. Still, local communities do have power, often more than they know. When the Montana ranchers and Native people stood together in front of the state legislature and at the U.S. Congress, they commanded attention. They spoke with authority because they are from, and of, the place that would be dynamited, excavated, and mined. And when it's their own backyard at stake, there is a fierceness about the activism, a willingness to do the hard work of poring over documents, mobilizing neighbors, and pressing for action from decision makers. There's also a willingness to reach out across barriers of race and culture to build the strength that can counter outside interests.

These communities become even more powerful as they develop their own vision for their future. Steve Charter believes that ranching that builds the ecological health of the soil can conserve scarce water resources, sequester carbon, enhance the productivity of the land, and create the foundation for a rural renaissance. He imagines a rebirth of small towns and land-based livelihoods as the labor-intensive techniques of restorative agriculture and ranching replace the chemical-intensive, soil-depleting, drought-intolerant techniques of agribusiness.

Likewise, the Native people I spoke to are relying on their treaty rights to protect the water resources and fisheries that can sustain future generations. As they restore their traditional ways, and bring in modern technologies and economies that suit their values, they are restoring their communities and becoming an increasingly powerful force for environmental protection.

Much of the focus of climate activism has been on national and international policy. But the local work is having a big impact. Restorative ranching, resistance to mining and fracking, and the protection of water and soil is best done by the people who live rooted in a place, rooted in relationships with others from that place, working out together how to be of and with a healthy, evolving ecosystem. I began to see the power of these people who know and care for their place and are willing to stand up for it.

Relationship to Earth/Place

A Culture of Connection	An Economy of Extraction
Restorative: We harvest but leave our place more alive and healthy than we found it.	*Extractive:* I profit by what I can take from the forests, water, and soil.
Earth, water, and life are sacred.	Natural resources are to be used to fuel our economy and build wealth.
Rooted: We are nourished by our place, and it supports us.	I am nimble and efficient, taking what I need and then moving on.
Our way of life and culture is informed by place.	*Exiled:* I can live anywhere but feel at home nowhere.
We are attached to our homes and resist displacement.	The market will determine who lives where, and who can afford a home.
Commons (water, air, climate stability, soil) belong to everyone, all beings, and all generations— it's our job to protect them.	Commons don't exist; every-thing is owned by individuals or government, or is available for dumping.
To be educated means to acquire deep learning about our place, including those aspects with no immediate benefit to humans.	Being well educated about a place means knowing how to efficiently extract its potential wealth.
We the people LOVE this place.	A romantic notion of place can interfere with an economy based on extracting value from land, water, forests, and soil.
Long-term well-being for generations to come is our responsibility, just as our ancestors provided that to us.	The corporate economy's time frame is short-term; the finance economy's is micro-seconds.
We look for ways to create livelihoods for upcoming generations, and value the vibrant communities that result.	Efficient, profitable economies replace human labor with technology; "community" has no economic value.

11. The Midwest

The Making of the Rust Belt

I drove southeast after leaving the Turtle Mountain Reservation, through Minnesota and then Wisconsin. The winding, two-lane highways through Amish communities and the small towns gave way to interstate highways. Towns became more frequent, then merged together into a nonstop grid of houses, malls, intersections, and gas stations. My GPS abruptly changed my route as I entered Chicago to avoid a traffic snarl as the evening rush hour began.

I felt daunted as I left behind the mountains and open prairies of the West and entered the congested city. I wondered where I would camp and how I would navigate the complex stories and relationships in these large cities. And how much hope could I expect to find? Many of those living in these cities have been beaten down for years by joblessness, disinvestment, poverty, and powerlessness.

My first stop in Chicago was at the Iron Street headquarters of Growing Power, an urban farm with five locations around the city, a food stand, and a training center for youth. At *YES!*, we had published articles about Growing Power and its founder,

Will Allen, the former NBA athlete who set up an organic farm in Milwaukee in 1993. Growing Power Chicago is run by his daughter, Erika Allen. Both organizations hire and train young people, 300 a year in Chicago alone.

Growing Power was hosting a conference of food justice advocates from throughout the Midwest while I was in Chicago, so I attended "Growing Food and Justice for All." Allen was in constant motion during the conference, one moment speaking to small groups of visitors, and the next, helping to grill up veggie kabobs and tofu. Like her father, she has a powerful physical presence, and when she speaks, things get done.

"We need to empower our young people who are being

Erika Allen leads Growing Power Chicago,
which hosted "Growing Food and Justice for All."

demonized and killed," Erika Allen said to those gathered at her urban farm. "There are high levels of trauma from living in this culture." The youth who work with Growing Power thrive in this environment, she said. "We don't have the resources to support the healing, but the gardens do that."

Chicago is known for a violent crime rate that is well above average, although 20 U.S. cities have a higher murder rate, according to the Pew Research Center.[1] More than a million city residents live in poverty, much of it concentrated in African American neighborhoods.[2]

For a time, Chicago and other Midwest cities were places where working-class people could get a job, own a home, and even put their children through college. In an economy that divided winners from losers, Midwesterners once counted themselves among the winners. That was when a job in a steel mill or auto factory was a ticket to the middle class, with security that extended into retirement and down through generations.

From the early part of the twentieth century through the 1960s, these cities were beacons to immigrants and to African Americans escaping Jim Crow laws and the vigilante terror of the Ku Klux Klan. Redlining, job discrimination, predatory lending, and official neglect of predominantly African American neighborhoods meant that black families were less likely to make it into the middle class, even when a family member landed a coveted manufacturing job. Still, some did make it, and the access to college gave the next generation a shot at a higher standard of living than their parents'.

But achieving a middle-class standard of living got harder. Wages stagnated, and families needed a second full-time income to get by as good-paying jobs disappeared. Technology replaced jobs, and union strength eroded as industry moved to nonunion states and overseas. NAFTA and other trade agree-

A mural from Growing Power, Chicago.

ments made it easy for companies to move production to low-wage countries with low environmental standards; with diminished import tariffs, companies could bring the products back to sell in the U.S. market.

Today's cities and states compete against each other for jobs, using massive public subsidies to lure corporations, pitting one impoverished city against another. The locally rooted economies are taxed to pay these corporate players, who may, or may not, stick around.

Corporations became less and less connected to any place—or any country. Companies won the global competition by extracting wealth from nature; from people, in the form of low wages; and from government, in the form of subsidies.

In this region, I was looking for signs that a successor to this extraction economy might be emerging. Given the impending climate crisis, it would have to be an economy that can function without further damage to the natural world. And given the shattering history of racial exclusion, it would have to be inclusive.

Growing Power in Chicago

The "Growing Food and Justice for All" conference began with a tour led by Tyres Walker, one of the dozens of mainly African American teenagers trained and employed at Growing Power. Walker, a wiry young man in a bright blue Growing Power T-shirt, showed us the warehouse that has the organization's offices upstairs and fish tanks, worm bins, and mushroom cultivation on the main floor, as well as a farm stand where produce and crafts are sold.

Behind the warehouse, next to the Chicago River, is the farm itself. Walker pulled open the doors to the hoop houses—half circles of piping that hold up sheets of plastic and keep the beds warm and productive—to show off the rows of vibrant lettuces and greens ready for harvest. Other vegetables were growing outside in raised beds, and goats and chickens were penned up nearby.

Walker described the trucks that pull up several times a week at Growing Power and dump piles of discarded fruit and vegetable waste. Other trucks deliver loads of wood chips. Layered together, these giant mounds break down into rich

Tyres Walker demonstrates Growing Power's composting techniques at a tour for participants of the "Growing Food and Justice for All" conference.

compost that, months later, crews shovel into vegetable beds. All told, the farm turns 450,000 pounds of waste into soil each year, allowing Growing Power to plant vegetables above Chicago's contaminated soil.

In many so-called food deserts, where boarded-up storefronts and payday lenders dominate, fresh food is hard to find. Liquor stores, gas stations, and bodegas are the only sources of food, and much of that is processed, loaded with sugar, and lacking nutrition. Several times a week, Growing Power crews load up a painted repurposed city bus with fresh fruits and vegetables and take it to places in those food deserts: schools, health centers, churches, and senior centers in Chicago's west and south sides.

People often think of food first when they start looking for ways to revitalize their communities. Residents establish community gardens, food co-ops, and food hubs; they grow food in school yards, parks, backyards, and indoor farms.

The local food economy also offers opportunities to entrepreneurs and immigrants, who start with little or nothing. Some begin with a food truck or vegetable stall; others sell a favorite soup or salsa at a farmers' market or by word of mouth. All of these activities connect people to each other and create livelihoods.

Food-related jobs in the extractive economy are another story. Farmworkers, meat processors, restaurant employees, and Walmart clerks are among the worst paid. According to the *Journal of Occupational and Environmental Medicine*, food laborers are most prone to injury, with high rates of illness and fatalities.[1]

The vision of the people attending the "Growing Food and Justice for All" conference is that the food system should pay a living wage and offer food that is healthy, culturally appropriate, and affordable. Furthermore, people who have been most

Painting a mural at the Growing Power urban farm in Chicago.

excluded from good-quality food and good-quality jobs should have the first chance to lead.

Walker's tour was over, and after an opening ceremony honoring the original Native American inhabitants of the land, the conference hosts lit a fire near the back corner of the property. Participants took turns keeping the fire burning throughout the three-day conference, creating a sacred and safe place. This shared responsibility and space served to acknowledge that trauma is a fact of life for many and that, just as we are working to restore soils and ecosystems, we also need healing and the reconnection that nourishes our souls.

Conference participants then got to work adding to the murals already begun on fences and warehouse walls, images that celebrated shiitake mushrooms and sweet potatoes, a girl facing a brilliant sunflower, a pair of dark brown bare feet with roots extending down through the rich earth to the water pooled below.

Food does much more than nourish our bodies. It connects us to our families—children who eat with their family regularly do better on all sorts of measures. It is at the center of celebrations and cultural events, so it connects us to our identity. And food connects us to place, to the soil and waters of where we live.

In the late afternoon, the farm staff laid out long tables, end to end, along the edge of the garden beds, lit candles, and brought dish after dish of fresh farm-raised food. Young staff members introduced themselves, their eyes bright in the candlelight. Each one—some shyly, some confidently—told the crowd, to applause and affirmation, about their plans and how they would use their training at Growing Power. Here, young people written off as destined for prison or a drive-by shooting are becoming, instead, the protagonists of their own future.

At New Era Windows, "We Work with Passion"

Leaving Chicago, I decided to drop in for a visit with a relatively new worker-owned manufacturing cooperative. My phone GPS guided me as I dodged trucks and potholes through the Brighton Park warehouse district. A hand-lettered sign above the loading dock said, "New Era Windows Cooperative." I asked at the office, and Armando Robles, one of the worker-owners, took time away from his work to talk.

Before it was a cooperative, the workers at what was then Republic Windows and Doors were simply told what to do, Robles told me. He had been a maintenance worker at Republic and president of United Electrical, Radio, and Machine Workers Local 1110. The workers there might have seen ways to improve the production process, but their supervisors weren't interested, he said.

"Whatever the bosses want, we do it. We'd say, 'Look, this is a better way,' and they'd say, 'No, we say you have to do it this way,'" explained Robles. "Even when they made a mistake, they just continued."

The situation is very different today. Employees of the New Era Windows Cooperative are also the owners. And their ideas matter. Anyone can propose improvements, and if that person convinces a majority of coworkers, things can change quickly.

"If we make a mistake, we talk to each other, and we find a solution," said Robles. "We try to do the best for everyone. We work harder because we're working for ourselves. But it's more enjoyable. We work with passion."

Each employee-owner has the opportunity to develop a wide range of capacities, instead of being confined to repetitive work while those at the top of the hierarchy make all the decisions and most of the money. Because workers are respected and heard, they tap into a resource previous owners had neglected—the smarts and creativity of the entire workforce.

Armando Robles and Beatriz Gurrola,
worker-owners of New Era Windows Cooperative.

Becoming a worker cooperative was a long journey, and it was a journey no one had planned. It began in the winter of 2008 when Republic's owners closed the factory and laid off the workforce without the required 60-days' notice. Workers occupied the factory and refused to leave the premises until they were paid what they were owed in severance pay and wages. Robles was one of the leaders of the occupation.

The story went nationwide. Pressure from the union, area activists, and even President Obama led to a victory: the workers were paid, and instead of shutting down, the factory was sold to California-based Serious Materials.

The workers kept their jobs, but the experience radicalized them. Several visited Argentina with Brendan Martin of The Working World, which, for some years, had been helping to finance worker-owned factories in that country. Robles and others from the Chicago company learned that workers facing the same situation had occupied their factories and eventually become worker-owners.

So Robles and his coworkers were prepared when, three years later, Serious Materials announced they would shut down and liquidate the factory. Once again, the workers occupied. With a nationwide petition drive, support from United Electrical Workers, financing from The Working World, backing from the local Occupy movement, and the memory of the previous occupation still fresh in the minds of the Chicago power elite, the protest turned into a buyout.

The New Era Windows Cooperative has been in operation since 2013, and the employees now run the business. It's been a steep learning curve. "It was difficult to make decisions together," Robles said. "But it's kind of fun, because at the end of the day it's for the benefit of everyone."

Sales are modest, but growing. There are 23 worker-owners,

and two staff members who Robles hopes will opt to become worker-owners.

How is this company staying alive when other owners have failed? The worker-owners made tough decisions to cut costs. They streamlined the products they offer, moved to a more affordable facility, and got rid of equipment that required costly upkeep. They did a lot of sales via word of mouth—the company prides itself on producing energy-efficient windows and doors customized to client specifications.

These worker-owners understood the challenge of competing with larger businesses that often get government subsidies and tax breaks or that operate in low-wage countries. Still, they have some advantages. Items that are heavy and expensive to transport, such as windows (and food), give local production an edge. Plus, "the good thing is we don't have the CEO making millions of dollars," Robles said, "so we can compete."

Instead of wealth being extracted from the work of New

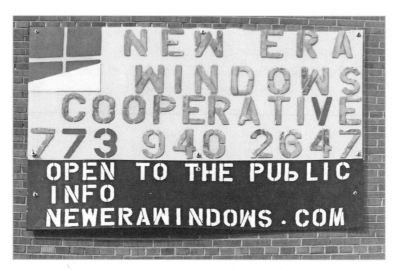

Sign at entrance to New Era Windows, Chicago.

Era employees, profits circulate back into the enterprise and into the workers' equity. The cooperative may not make the big profits of companies producing in low-wage regions, but it offers other sorts of returns, such as steady employment and work that provides dignity and opportunities to grow professionally. New Era also offers the security that comes from being part of a community that cares about many values—including the common good. That community came out to help the workers when they were occupying the factory and later during the buyout. And they give back by making environmentally sound products.

New Era's worker-ownership model offers something else: it's based on "enough." Enough pay and benefits to live with dignity. Enough production machinery, but not the sort that is too expensive. Enough profits to reinvest in the company, but worker-owners are free of the burden of producing high and growing profits to satisfy absentee shareholders. The Working World's "patient" financing put the priority on the success of the cooperative, not on large or rapid returns. This sense of "enough" counters the impulse to extract and degrade. Instead, this cooperative has created a model for abundance and shared prosperity.

A statement on their website suggests they know that their workplace is revolutionary: "Like all U.S. pioneers, the paths we blaze are open for other adventuring souls to follow, and we look forward to being part of the next renaissance of 'made in America.'"

The Detroiters Who Are Redefining Prosperity

The drive to Detroit on the interstate is much like other drives through the Midwest: long expanses of highway, punctuated by overpasses and truck stops.

As you enter Detroit, though, the decay soon becomes glaring. The old Michigan Central Train Station, formerly a grand landmark for the city and the tallest train station in the world, has been empty since the last Amtrak train left in 1988. Today, its dark windows symbolize the decline of a once great city. Elsewhere, the old Packard auto plant has turned into a much-photographed site—the manufacturing complex now in ruins, festooned with graffiti and spray-painted art, windows gone, grass and trees growing through the concrete and breaking up the three-story buildings. Other less imposing structures in the city also slide slowly into collapse. Some blocks contain burned-out shells of houses, while nearby, families go on with their lives.

Detroit's auto industry was a major magnet for workers during its manufacturing boom. But the jobs left, and white flight along with government disinvestment left many black workers and their families with little but predatory lenders, liquor stores, and drug traffickers. Today, Detroit is a city of widespread evictions and water shutoffs—a city that, until recently, was famous for Devil's Night, a Halloween tradition, when hundreds of fires were set throughout the city.

I came, though, not to marvel at the decay. I came because I have visited Detroit for a number of years, and each time I have learned about what it means to, as Grace Lee and Jimmy Boggs said, "make a way out of no way." The people I have met in Detroit have thought long and hard about change. I always discover something here about where we are in history and about what is possible for Detroit, and for us as a species.

Myrtle Denise Thompson and Wayne Curtis live in a pleasant home with a welcoming front porch filled with toys for their grandchildren. Their neighborhood, though, is a mix of vacant lots, abandoned houses, and occupied homes. Several years ago, they planted the vacant lot next door with a big community garden they call the Feedom Freedom Garden. It's a tough neighborhood, and people tend to keep to themselves, but the garden brought people out of their homes, as they shared gardening tasks and the fruits and vegetables. When a neighbor across the street was threatened with foreclosure, the Curtis family, neighbors, and friends gathered to support her.

Curtis and Thompson took me outside to show what happened next.

In order to evict her, the neighbors believed, a dumpster would have to be set at the house so the eviction crew could throw out her belongings. Curtis, Thompson, and other members of the eviction defense group built a fence on the empty lot next door so there would be no place to put the dumpster. Supporters declared themselves ready to come out at a moment's notice if the eviction crew showed up.

Once the fence was built, the neighbors, including kids, painted it with designs and words about what was on their minds.

"We need a village," Curtis said as he gestured toward the fence.

The fence is about six feet high, made up of various segments of wooden boards, some vertical and some horizontal. It is covered with brightly colored illustrations and slogans: Black Homes Matter, Wage Love, Say Her Name, Foreclosure Free Zone, Ain't we got a right to the tree of life, We want black families, black neighborhoods, free of foreclosures and water shutoffs and police brutality.

A giant snail is labeled "Caracol of resistencia," a shout-out to Zapatista communities in southern Mexico and, coincidentally, the name of my camper. The neighborhood children painted images of people along the bottom of the fence, and Curtis noted that the next round of illustrations would be of gay

Neighbors created this fence to try to stop an eviction.

people who have been killed over the years, not by police but by other members of the community.

Curtis has graying, nearly waist-length dreadlocks gathered behind his back.

"Individualism works under capitalism—you can buy your way or pay for what you need. But we're dispensable, marginal, because we don't have money," Curtis said. "So for us, the transformation comes out of collective work. We need resistance, but we also need healing and rebuilding."

Many talk of a renaissance happening in Detroit, and there are two very different ideas about what that means. Some people mean the sort of thing Curtis and Thompson are doing, growing food and connecting with neighbors. For others, though, the rebirth is about the new boutique hotels, craft beer outlets, and upscale restaurants, located downtown, evidence that the old Detroit of wealth and whiteness is back.

The longtime Detroiters I talked to say the big investments are for newcomers who work for one of the corporations located downtown, like Quicken Loans, which is among the largest mortgage lenders in the United States. They point out that, while money is pouring into the business core, little is trickling down to the vast, underpopulated, overwhelmingly African American neighborhoods, such as the one where the Curtis family lives.

Forbes declared Detroit the nation's most dangerous city in 2015, with a murder rate 10 times the national average.[1] *Time* magazine declared it the poorest,[2] with nearly 40 percent of the population living below the poverty line. The population has dropped by more than half since its height of 1.8 million in 1950. Despite the abundance of houses, both empty and occupied, poor families are losing their homes to bank and tax foreclosures. And despite the abundance of fresh water from the Great

Lakes, the city has some of the highest water rates in the country and a policy of massive water shutoffs for those behind in their bills. The city, meanwhile, committed to spending $400 million on a third major sports arena, even while it was in bankruptcy.

William Copeland, Climate Justice Director at the Eastern Michigan Environmental Council and a hip-hop artist, thinks a lot about how, in the face of all the challenges, the people of Detroit can have a say over what happens in their city. "Right now, we're defining our power in the face of displacement, in the face of gentrification, in the face of other people's plans for Detroit," he told me when I ran into him at a justice march. Copeland is tall and lanky, and he was wearing a blue stocking cap to ward off the cold wind as we walked through downtown Detroit.

"I think we get power from our culture, which is one way we define ourselves," he said. "When we know our culture and we're rooted in our culture, we know ourselves, and it becomes much more difficult for other people's goals or other things that aren't in our interest to motivate us or to sway us."

That same spirit of resistance and celebration, organizing and community, infuses many of the projects I visited. The Detroit Black Community Food Security Network operates a small farm within the city, teaching young people about growing food and raising bees and farm animals, and distributing fresh food in some of the city's food deserts.

In Highland Park, a small, impoverished enclave within the boundaries of the city, a group calling itself Soulardarity installed two solar-powered streetlights when the city removed streetlights to save money. "These streetlights demonstrate a different story about what clean energy is all about," Jackson Koeppel, one of the founders, said. "It can be green, community owned, and sustainable."

Julia Putnam, a young mother and a protégée of Grace Lee

Julia Putnam, co-founder and principal of the
James and Grace Lee Boggs School in Detroit.

Boggs, started an elementary school where students, whom she
calls *solutionaries*, are encouraged to use their imagination, to
extend their interests outside the classroom, and to consider
what is possible for their community. The idea is to give them a
deep grounding in their own culture and identity while taking
them into the neighborhoods, where they learn about the history and ecology of their surrounds.

Reverend Joan Ross is working to create a land trust so
that especially important stretches of the boulevards through
Detroit's African American neighborhoods have a shot at
community-controlled revitalization. She's also working on a
low-power FM radio station. She and others managed to ac-
quire a license to broadcast, and she figures they can reach
300,000 people in the seven-mile radius of the transmission
tower. People who don't have a voice will be heard, if this project gets up and running.

During my week in Detroit, I spoke with people who were involved in building windmills out of spare parts and mobilizing the city's Latino community to resist violence and to celebrate its culture. No single venture alone was transformative, but together, they showed that people working creatively and persistently, against powerful odds, were creating the city and the world they wanted to live in.

The legacy of Grace Lee and Jimmy Boggs

This broad-based leadership—the willingness to step up and make change, and to make it celebratory change—is, in no small part, a result of the influence of James and Grace Lee Boggs. The two were at the center of many of the city's social justice movements beginning in the mid-1950s. Grace, the daughter of Chinese immigrants, was one of the first Asian American women to earn a PhD from Bryn Mawr; Jimmy, an African American autoworker who had moved to Detroit from Alabama, was a self-taught intellectual, writer, and speaker. The two of them engaged the city's African American community in a deep reflection on the state of the world, the character of the times, and the most effective ways of making change. Their insistence that we not only resist harmful institutions and practices but also envision and build the world we want has influenced generations of leaders. As a young activist, I had eagerly read their books and articles, and I heard them speak once when they visited Portland, Oregon.

Jimmy Boggs died in 1993, but Grace continued her activism for many years after his death, always reminding colleagues and friends of their own potential for leadership, and always provoking them to think profoundly and strategically about history and change. People, especially social justice activists, visited her from all over. Her question "What time is it on the clock of the world?" remains at the center of the conversation among activists influenced by the Boggses, in Detroit and beyond.

Any trip I take to Detroit includes a stop at the Boggs Center, an activists' facility named after the couple, which carries on the tradition of deep conversations and working for change. A banner on the wall there reads, "From growing the economy to growing our souls."

And I always try to see Grace Lee Boggs, although this visit was especially poignant. Grace had recently turned 100. She lived on the ground floor of the two-story house she and Jimmy lived in for decades; the Boggs Center is on the second floor.

"She may or may not recognize you," Richard Feldman, a former United Auto Worker activist and member of the Boggs Center board, told me when I met there with other board members.

I was ushered into her small bedroom, and Grace did recognize me. We held hands and spoke briefly; she asked after mutual friends. The last time I had visited her, only a year earlier, I'd left knowing that could be our last conversation. This time, that seemed even more likely. Her eyes were watery, her hand felt light, and her skin was transparent. Propped up in her bed, she was attended by caretakers 24 hours a day.

Three days later, she passed away. I was on the other side of Detroit when I heard. The impromptu memorial that evening brought dozens of her friends and admirers to the Boggs Center—young and old, people who had known and loved her for years, some whose lives had been shaped by her and Jimmy. In the modest brick home where the two of them had lived, people gathered from around the city to tell stories of her life, read poems, sing, laugh, and mourn. By the end of the evening, candles were lined up along the path to the front porch and up and down the sidewalk.

The legacy continues

Halima Cassells, a woman young enough to have been Grace's great-granddaughter, is living out many of the ideas that are promoted at the Boggs Center. During my weeklong visit, I kept running into this artist and mother of two, who was born and raised in Detroit. Once was at a roundtable hosted by an art gallery, which she attended with her daughter and her mother, where all were invited to participate in what turned out to be a profound exploration of the meaning of sustainable economics. Cassells was also part of a monthly food justice dinner and celebration I attended, and I saw her again at the Boggs Center. I asked her if we could talk, and we agreed to meet at the Avalon Bakery.

Cassells is slight, with a long face, short-cropped hair, and a quiet, thoughtful intelligence. She works with some of Detroit's most innovative organizations, including Incite Focus, a fabrication laboratory (fab lab). Its goals are, according to a statement on their website, to "work and spend less, create and connect more." Incite Focus strives for "ecological benefits—emit and degrade less; human benefits—enjoy and thrive more."

At the fab lab, students learn digital fabrication, permaculture, experiential learning, and appropriate technology, and how to combine them. They use 3-D printers and computer-aided design to make anything from an iPhone case to an electronic circuit to multipurpose furniture that can be taken apart and put together for a different function. The lab's tools for flexible manufacturing allow users to create a prototype for a business venture or a one-off for personal use.

Halima Cassells at the Avalon Bakery in Detroit.

Incite Focus is also designing and building net zero-energy homes that produce their own solar energy and grow their own food, and the group hopes to cluster eight to ten of them into intentional communities.

The skills learned in the fab lab can prepare users for all sorts of high-tech jobs. But the aim of the lab is more about channeling creativity and about learning how to meet your needs and those of family and friends. Making you less reliant on a job frees up time and the psychic space to create the sort of life—and the sort of world—that works for you and your neighbors.

But that's just one of the places where Cassells spends her time. She also works with the Center for Community-Based Enterprise, a Detroit-based organization that helps launch cooperatives and other forms of worker ownership nationwide.

In addition, she's involved in a bunch of DIT (do-it-together) activities. She organizes swaps, where, for example, families of schoolchildren can exchange outgrown winter clothes for those that are the right size. Her membership in a time bank, along with the memberships of more than a hundred others, means she can trade her time and art for help in getting her rambling home fixed up. So she can do less of the tasks she dislikes, like filling out paperwork, she said, and more of the things she loves, like connecting people and throwing art parties. The combination of some paid work, some exchange, and some doing things herself adds up to a livelihood.

She has no illusions about the challenges of living in a city where foreclosures, water shutoffs, arson, and displacement make life a challenge for most residents. She compared the treatment of Detroit's African American majority to the treatment of communities in the way of corporate profits in Third World countries. There, the issue is gold, chocolate, diamonds, and coffee. "They deal with more overt violence," she said.

"But the effect is the same when you tell a 90-year-old woman, 'We're going to shut off your water because you owe 150 dollars,' and the bill might not even be right!" she said. "There are so many questions about bills, and those bills are grounds for essentially removing you from your home. In this game of capitalism, the removal of people is for short-term gain. The most effective thing is to always keep people in survival mode."

Cassells had suggested we meet at Avalon Bakery, a coffee shop in a neighborhood that had no such gathering places until it was launched by two women who were inspired by the Boggs Center's vision of a revitalized Detroit. When they first opened, they were advised to keep the windows small and covered with bars because of the area's high crime rate. They did the opposite. The bakery has enormous windows that reach nearly to the high ceilings, inside and outside tables, and an entrance that invites all comers.

Cassells told a story from the food justice dinner we had both attended a few days before at the Cass Corridor Commons. There, delicious meals made from fresh, local food are offered free to the community one Friday a month. The night I was there, groups of people clustered around tables painting signs for a justice rally happening the next day in downtown Detroit. Others shared their meals, laughing and talking. Music producer and activist Bryce Detroit emceed an open mic, with children and adults offering songs, spoken word, and dance to applause and shout-outs from the crowd.

"Were you there at the end?" Cassells asked me. I hadn't been. I'd left after a couple of hours to attend another event before heading back to my host's home.

"All the kids in the entire space, from age 14 on down to barely walking, got up in front and did the Whip and the Nae Nae," she said, laughing. "Everyone was cheering and dancing along!"

I asked Cassells how she would describe the sort of world she is working to create. She looked thoughtful and then said something I hadn't expected in this troubled city: "I'm kind of there. My life is pretty awesome, pretty overjoyed, and I'm in gratitude at some point every day."

As we talked, people streamed into the bakery for coffee or a loaf of fresh-baked bread, and several of them, when they saw Cassells, smiled and waved. "Like this," she noted. "We're supporting each other. I would just like to bring more people along."

In a sprawling, 137-square-mile depopulated city, where poverty and hardships are ever present, the creativity and common purpose, love and mutual support, are producing a sense of abundance and new possibilities.

Dr. Garcia, Gunshot Wounds, and a Plea for Jobs in Cincinnati

Cincinnati is one of the fastest-growing cities in the Midwest. Corporate giants such as Procter & Gamble and Kroger are headquartered there, and some of its close-in neighborhoods have become chic, with coffee shops and new condominiums. But, as in Detroit, downtown prosperity is not trickling down to the poorest, predominantly African American residents, who are more likely to get displaced by the new condos than to own one.

Cincinnati is among the most segregated cities in the United States, Dr. Victor Garcia, a trauma surgeon at Cincinnati Children's Hospital, told me when we met for coffee. Child poverty is second only to Detroit. Studies show that concentrated poverty is associated with increases in hypertension in children as young as six years old, he said. Life expectancy differs by 20 years between neighborhoods within a half mile of one another.

Garcia is a soft-spoken, middle-aged African American doctor with graying hair at the temples and intense eyes. We met at a busy downtown breakfast spot. I arrived early and saw that he was in an intense conversation with his earlier

Dr. Victor Garcia, a pediatric surgeon in Cincinnati.

appointment—city officials, he told me later. He finished up that meeting and joined me at a booth, and then filled me in on how he had come to rethink his life work as a pediatrician when he saw that health—survival, even—for young African Americans in his community would take more than access to medical treatment.

"I'm seeing more and more kids coming in with gunshot wounds," he said. "In these neighborhoods, you see the equivalence of the PTSD that you see in veterans coming back from war."

This level of violence is a public health emergency and a moral failure, in his view. He made a pledge to take action when a 14-year-old girl died in his arms of a gunshot wound. She was just the latest of many young victims of gun violence he had treated; the number in Cincinnati rose 300 percent over 10 years, he told me. Their average age is 12.9 years old. Dr. Garcia told the girl's mother he would do everything in his power to make sure he'd never have to tell another mother that her daughter had died from a cause that is so clearly preventable.

"Violence is a symptom," he said, "as is infant mortality and premature birth." All are symptoms of multigenerational poverty. The real key to preventing childhood death is to create new ways that people can earn living wages in the urban core, he said.

To compete with global corporations that produce in low-wage regions, a business needs to be locally rooted. Cooperatives or similar structures in which workers have an ownership share of the business work best in these communities, he believes.

"If people have skin in the game, they are more likely to stay with it and more likely to leverage their genius to making it more productive," he said.

One idea for Cincinnati? Grow microgreens inside, under lights, in abandoned buildings in the inner city. One such venture, Waterfields, is operating now. The company delivers trays of live greens to high-end restaurants. These microgreens are flavorful and popular with chefs.

The business is tiny, but Dr. Garcia believes there is potential. What if the big "anchor institutions" in the city, like the hospitals and schools, committed to buying all the produce they could from local companies like Waterfields? You'd create sustainable jobs not only for those enterprises but also for the businesses that serve them—day-care centers for the children of company employees, for example. Clusters of businesses are needed to begin bringing a neighborhood out of poverty, he said.

By growing locally, you could take on two of our most pressing crises—inequality and climate change, he said. You could reduce the carbon impact of growing vegetables, plus employ people with low skills or no skills. And because they would be co-owners, this model would help restore their sense of pride.

Dr. Garcia is inspired by the example of the Evergreen Co-operatives in Cleveland. There, area hospitals, a local foundation, a couple of universities, and a national organization dedicated to local wealth building—the Democracy Collaborative—formed the Evergreen Cooperatives to address exactly these sorts of issues. A worker-owned laundry caters to these large anchor institutions, supplying jobs in poor neighborhoods.

This is the dream Dr. Garcia hopes to bring to Cincinnati. Reconnecting the economy to the community can mean living-wage jobs and restoring hope and agency for people who have been left out. Clustering jobs helps the vitality ripple out, so the expenditures of one business can provide a customer base for other businesses.

Jane Jacobs and Michael Shuman: why local, not global, economies

How much potential is there to bring back prosperous local economies—and to make them just, inclusive, and green? Writer and urban activist Jane Jacobs is well known for up-ending the conventional wisdom on urban design, which had favored high-rise apartments and freeways that demolished long-standing neighborhoods. Her books illustrate the importance of human-scale design and the sense of community that develops when people regularly encounter each other on busy streets. Cities are complex and decentralized, she shows, and they operate best when they work like diverse emergent ecosystems.

Jacobs is less well known for her ideas about human-scale economics and how to revive the economies of cities. Among other things, she has written about "import substitution": Replace items bought from outside the metropolitan area with items manufactured, grown, or processed within the city, and you boost local hiring. The people who land these jobs then have money to spend, and if they can spend at least some of their income with other local producers, the effects continue to ripple out into a virtuous cycle of prosperity.

Unfortunately, most cities do not take this approach.

"The problem is that economic development professionals have naked self-interest," economist and author Michael Shuman told me when I asked him about this later. "Bringing one big [corporate] player to town makes page-one news; it's good for their career and for the politicians they serve. The fact that it has nothing to do with the economic vitality of the community is irrelevant."

It gets worse. We need to realize that much of what is traditionally considered "economic development" undermines the local economy, Shuman said. These approaches take tax money from all of us, including small and medium-sized business owners, and give it to big corporations in the form of subsidies and tax breaks. This undermines job creation, since small and medium-sized businesses—not giant transnational corporations—create two thirds of all new jobs in the United States.[1]

Likewise, subsidies to big coal, big oil, big cattle, big agribusiness, and other extractive industries all tip the balance against small and medium-sized, locally rooted businesses. Because big companies exert outsized influence in government, subsidies for the extractive economy continue at the national and local levels, and as they do, they undermine the local economy, ecological sustainability, and community stability.

The outcome of this lopsided power is evident in all parts of our lives. Deregulated Wall Street banks bet recklessly on the mortgage industry and millions lose their homes and, in many cases, their entire net worth. Exxon lies about climate-change science and spends millions to promote those lies, and action on the climate crisis is delayed by decades. BP pollutes the Gulf of Mexico with a giant oil spill. Massey Energy blows up mountaintops. Companies close their factory doors to move to non-union states where wages are low, and then close those factories to move abroad to where wages are even lower. Furthermore, these companies and their wealthy executives use their lopsided power to win tax cuts for themselves and impose austerity budgets for everyone else. Local governments find themselves in budget crises, unable to maintain basic services, much less to help the poor get a fresh start when their homes and jobs are taken away.

Bringing our economies home is one of the most important ways to restore democracy and to bring vitality, ecological sustainability, and self-determination to our communities.

Americans get it. Two thirds of them (67 percent, according to a 2015 Gallup poll[2]) have confidence in small business—the highest percentage for any U.S. institution except the military. Big business and banks, in contrast, are trusted by only 21 percent of Americans.[3]

What is less clear is how to bring economic power home.

The Union Movement's Hail Mary Pass

In the decades after World War II, the union movement was one of the main forces boosting the incomes and security of working people. In fact, there would probably be no middle class in the United States without it.[1] But the number of union members peaked in 1979, and unions have been fighting losing battles since then against the increasing power of globalized corporations.

Some people are trying something different: unionized worker-owned cooperatives.

"So many times we're on the defensive, we're reacting," Ellen Vera, a staff organizer with the United Food and Commercial Workers (UFCW), told me. Vera was on loan from the UFCW, working with a diverse group of people in Cincinnati to jump-start a new effort to create unionized worker-owned cooperatives.

Unionized cooperatives "give us a way to proactively create the kind of work environment we really want to see."

I met Ellen and her husband, Flequer Vera, at a small restaurant in Cincinnati, along with Kristen Barker, executive director of the Cincinnati Union Co-op Initiative.

"After the recession, we all lost money; the banks got the money after they ruined us," said Flequer Vera, an immigrant from Peru, who grew up working in his family's construction business. Flequer became involved in social justice issues because of his own precarious status as an undocumented worker and out of his concern for formerly incarcerated people.

"We were studying alternatives," he explained. "When I learned about Mondragon, I saw an opportunity to merge my passions for community organizing, social justice, and community development with my passion for business."

Flequer Vera, founder of Sustainergy, was inspired by the Mondragon cooperatives of Spain.

The Mondragon Cooperative is a large and successful worker-owned cluster of 260 enterprises employing 74,000 people. The cooperatives began in the postwar Basque region of Spain as a way to provide jobs at a time when the region was deeply impoverished. The well-being of people and the community is, according to the group's website, Mondragon's only goal.

Flequer Vera was one of those inspired by Mondragon; his project is Sustainergy, a cooperative that retrofits homes to improve their energy efficiency. Sustainergy creates well-paying jobs in low-income communities; workers can pick up the needed skills relatively quickly, Flequer said. The co-op helps the environment by reducing energy use. And homeowners save hundreds of dollars a year on their energy bills.

Sustainergy is just one of the projects of the Cincinnati Union Co-op Initiative, originally created in 2009 as a partnership between Mondragon and the United Steelworkers.

Ellen Vera sees worker cooperatives as a way to complement job-site labor organizing. She told me the story of Ezekiel (Zeke) Coleman, whom I had met earlier at Our Harvest Food Hub, another project of the Union Co-op Initiative. Coleman, now a worker-owner at Our Harvest, had been an employee at a chicken processing plant and a key leader in a union organizing drive there, she told me. "He was awesome and fought really hard trying to organize." But then, as often happens during organizing drives, he got fired. "It's so hard to see people getting crushed when they try to stand up," Ellen said.

She introduced him to Our Harvest, which has its own farms in and near Cincinnati and—via its food hub—distributes produce to wholesale and individual customers. A new approach Our Harvest recently began developing is to deliver fresh produce at wholesale rates to more than a dozen community centers, churches, low-income housing projects, and

Kristen Barker heads up the Cincinnati Union Co-op Initiative, with Christopher DeAngelis, general manager of Apple Street Co-op, outside the co-op's soon-to-be-refurbished building.

day-care centers. These organizations mark up the prices to retail levels and use the difference to fund their own projects. New Jerusalem Baptist Church used the money raised this way to fund a tour of historically black colleges for prospective students, Barker told me.

Now Coleman is both a co-op worker-owner at Our Harvest and a member of the co-op's board of directors. Based on our brief conversation, he's happy with his new status: "This is more like a family atmosphere, working together with everybody, getting to know everybody," he said. "It's not like a normal warehouse job. It's a lot less stressful."

The Cincinnati Union Co-op Initiative has another big project in the works: a worker- and community-owned cooperative grocery store planned for an area that lacks access to good-quality food.

The Apple Street Co-op got off to a rocky start. This cooperative will be located in what is now a vacant grocery store building in a low-income area, where residents will be looking more for affordable prices than for organic labels. The organizers initially doubted that they could make the finances work. But with careful budgeting and the support of 1,150 people who have signed up to be community member-owners, the project is moving ahead, according to Barker. Renovation of the old grocery store was set to begin in late 2016.

I left Cincinnati in October, and in November the Union Co-op Initiative brought together 150 people from around the United States and from Mondragon to spread the union–co-op model. I checked in with Barker for an update as I was completing work on this book, and she called me back from Spain, where she was on a delegation touring the Mondragon cooperatives.

More unions have joined the effort since we talked, she told me. The United Auto Workers; the American Federation of State, County and Municipal Workers; the International Union of Electronic, Electrical, Salaried, Machine, and Furniture Workers–Communications Workers of America; the American Federation of Teachers; and the United Steelworkers are all involved. Manufacturing is a major focus of the Union Co-op Initiative's efforts.

There are union–co-op initiatives now based in Los Angeles, Greater Dayton, Nashville, New York, Chicago, and Colorado. The Cincinnati group is offering classes on how to get union–co-ops going, and the idea is spreading.

Another piece of good news: the delegation that Barker was traveling with was largely made up of credit union managers. A number of existing cooperatives were funded by their local credit union, she told me—which is not surprising, since credit unions are cooperatives themselves. If credit unions step up their lending to this form of local economic enterprise, union-co-ops could take off. The Small Business Administration is also making loans more accessible to cooperatives, she added.

Another factor could help the model spread. Four million businesses in the United States are owned by baby boomers who will be retiring in coming years, and only a small percentage of those businesses will be taken over by family members.[2] Ellen Vera is encouraging such business owners to consider selling their enterprises to employees when they retire. "There's a way you could keep all these people employed who have invested so much time," she tells business owners. "Turn it into a worker co-op."

Numerous potential routes may lead to a surge of cooperative economics: labor unions, credit unions, community groups, and baby boomer business owners are all contributing.

The faith community is also engaged. In Cincinnati, several faith groups have formed The Economics of Compassion Initiative, based on the idea that a religious concern about poverty requires action to transform the economy. This group has been exploring alternative economic systems in which workers and owners share benefits, the community is enhanced, and justice is a priority. One possibility is that the community will declare a Jubilee Year in 2019. What that would mean, exactly, was unclear at the time I was visiting. But in the Old Testament, the Jubilee was a time to cancel debts, free the enslaved, and return (redistribute) the land. Such restorative actions would be welcome in today's society, with the high levels of debt, human trafficking and mass incarcerations, and extreme and growing inequality.

Community Work for Community Good

PROSPECT, KENTUCKY—I was pretty sure I had never been to Kentucky. I thought about that as I once again got lost. I had taken it on faith that my phone GPS would get me and my truck-camper where I wanted to go.

I was trying to get to La Minga, a small farm cooperative founded by Central American immigrants. A harvest festival was under way, and I was rushing to get there before it ended.

I had passed through the city of Louisville, out into the suburbs, past fall-colored trees, and creeks and lakes, and housing developments, puzzling about where a farm could be among the strip malls and cul-de-sacs. The GPS took me into a little neighborhood of tract houses and then declared I had arrived. No farm in sight.

I backtracked, found the turnoff I'd missed, and parked my truck-camper alongside cars and trucks next to a farmhouse. There, people were filling plates with beans, homemade tamales, and a salad of greens fresh-picked from just a few feet away. I did the same and then sat on a hay bale and talked to a few of the other visitors. Soon a band started to play on the front porch of the farmhouse. A few couples began to dance. Children and grown-ups commenced a pick-up soccer game in the open field beyond the house. And I got to meet the founders.

La Minga was established by Nelson Escobar, originally from El Salvador, who began growing his favorite foods from home when he first arrived in Kentucky. He originally planted 25 different crops, but keeping up with that much variety became too much work. Escobar is not only a farmer but also an experienced community organizer, so he recruited others to farm—immigrants like himself as well as native-born Americans. At the celebration, he circulated, talking to many of the guests.

Nelson Escobar, originally from El Salvador, founded La Minga.

"Because we're humans, doing work together is really sat-isfying," he told me. "Each person says which three things they will sow. Then they share the harvest with others." Escobar grows potatoes, jicama, and greens.

Elmer Zavala, originally from Honduras, also farms at La Minga. Zavala, wearing a blue-and-white soccer jersey and a broad straw hat with a red bandana around it, grew up helping his father work to raise crops on their small farm. But when it came time to harvest, prices inevitably would have dropped.

"When I came to this country, I didn't want to go into ag-riculture," Zavala said. "For years, I looked for another liveli-hood, because I didn't want to follow my father's path." But he missed the foods of home and decided he would cultivate them here.

"What I really love about this is the collective," Zavala said. "I love sharing the harvest. And when we grow it ourselves, we don't have to worry that our food was grown in conditions that exploit workers."

La Minga means "community work for community good" in the indigenous Aymara language, he told me.

The group farms on about 15 acres, with plots of land di-vided among the farmers. Three members of the collective plan to raise fish and vegetables in a small greenhouse, where they have installed experimental aquaponics tanks. Their ambition is to take their model to schools and to urban areas where con-taminated soil and sparse land make growing food difficult.

Carla Wallace, a middle-aged woman with dark brown hair, owns the property and loans it to the cooperative. "I believe we live in a country in which the land is concentrated in the hands of a few rich people, and there are a lot of people who need to farm and do not have access to land," she said. "To me, with all this acreage we have, to be able to provide this land to the farm-

Stephen Lewis, Sunita Deobhakta, and Priyanka Deobhakta inside a La Minga greenhouse.

ers, that's a gift to us instead of the other way around. In some tiny way, it evens the scales a little bit."

Although the land is hers, she doesn't decide how it's managed. "I think it's important that the people who are making the decisions here are a diverse mix of folks. It's not being done for people; people are doing and leading it themselves. I'm not on the board; I don't get a vote, and I think that's how it should be."

Nelson now lives in the farmhouse where Wallace used to live—she has moved into town. She sometimes farms, she said, but her effort to raise sweet potatoes made her appreciate how difficult farmwork is.

As we talked, the music picked up on the porch, and more couples joined the dance on the grass out front. More people arrived and helped themselves to tamales. The free-form soccer game continued, young kids and adults running and laughing on the field by the greenhouse.

Here in Kentucky these farmers don't have the multigenerational relationship to the land that they had back home in Central America. In the context of partisan politics, their status as immigrants would make them suspect. But they have consciously chosen to build connections—to link people together, to grow and share food that keeps them tied to their culture and creates a bond to their adopted home. Their harvest consists of not only fresh produce but also the sense of community and abundance that comes with shared effort and celebration.

An economy with future

Traveling through the Midwest, I didn't find one simple answer to the poverty and racial exclusion that beset this region. What answers I did find are not even close to the scale needed.

Still, people are experimenting with a better design for the economy. Many turn first to food because it reconnects us to our own bodies and health, to our cultures and celebrations, to one another when we break bread together, and to the earth.

Cooperatives offer those who have been excluded from the economy the chance to own a share of it. The DIT (do-it-together) informal economy joins people and turns waste into treasures. The arts and culture offer more entry points to this new economy and remind us that the economy isn't simply about producing and accumulating stuff—it's also the celebration of the human spirit.

A culture of connection is emerging in parts of these cities as people redefine what is important and put their commitment to their place, and to each other, ahead of the extraction and

Part of the harvest at La Minga.

consumerism of the old economy. The values and concerns I found as I traveled were remarkably consistent—people know that the next generation of enterprises must not only stop damaging the natural environment but also be restorative. And the old divides between winners and losers, between haves and have-nots, between white people who own and run things and people of color who are consigned to poverty—those are over.

I found an extraordinary group of local leaders who are developing this new economic ethos, and with it they are bringing a joyful sense of abundance and sharing into everyday life.

The tug-of-war between the extractive economy and the place-based economy is happening all over the world. In the United States, economist and author Michael Shuman told me, a huge bottleneck to thriving local economies is finance. The pensions and savings of the very people harmed by the extractive economy are still flowing into stocks and bonds of the companies doing the most damage. If we can divert that investment to local entrepreneurs, land trusts, cooperatives, local renewable-energy companies, credit unions, and so forth, we may see local, just, sustainable economies take off.

Relationship to Our Economies

A Culture of Connection	An Economy of Extraction
Real wealth is human, community, ecological well-being.	Real wealth is money that is liquid and can be extracted and concentrated in a few hands.
Societies flourish when wealth is widely distributed and circulates locally.	Wealth rewards merit, and the concentration of wealth allows investment.
An economy of cooperation creates a place for everyone.	Capitalism creates big financial rewards for the winners.
Relationships come first: self, family, community, place, environment.	Money comes first, which, managed well, offers a small group of people a good life.
Invest in long-term well-being of the whole.	Put money into financial instruments that enhance private gain.
Invest in infrastructure and the commons.	Privatize everything—that's where efficiency and profit lie.
Internalize costs—the full costs to people, community, and environment should be included in the price; share benefits.	Externalize costs—transfer expenses to government, the community, or nature to keep prices low; privatize benefits.
Food and water are more important.	Oil and gas are more lucrative.
Work for a sustainable prosperity.	Boom, and then move on.
Keep it local, so the full range of human and ecological values are considered.	Keep it global, so wealth can efficiently concentrate.
Climate change represents a huge challenge—we all need to pitch in.	Climate change is a problem for someone else, or future generations, to solve.

This chart is influenced by the work of my longtime colleague David Korten, especially *Agenda for a New Economy: From Phantom Wealth to Real Wealth* (Berrett-Koehler Publishers, 2010).

III. The East

Appalachia's Coalfields Extraction

Two men wearing camouflage and orange caps looked up and waved as I drove down a back road in my snail-painted camper. Confederate flags festooned both the fronts of sad trailers perched precariously above the road and the large, well-appointed brick homes that sat proudly above acres of mowed grass.

I was on my way to the coalfields of Kentucky. The landscape of this region, like Montana's, has been devastated by the fossil fuel extraction economy; like the Midwest Rust Belt cities, the area has experienced a long-standing economic depression; and, like African American communities throughout the country, it has been marginalized and isolated.

The media often ridicules the people of Appalachia as hillbillies, impoverished, and ignored, although their elected officials claim to stand up for them and for coal companies.

This state also makes the list of the country's top ten most racist states.

Who in this region, I wondered, was charting a path for the future? And is there a link between communities that are rebuilding their sense of self-worth and the quality of those communities' relationships to peoples of different races?

I was on my way to Whitesburg, Kentucky, to see what I could find out. But first, I had to find a place to camp for the night.

WYTHEVILLE, VIRGINIA—The park keeper at the campsite looked at me skeptically as she checked me in, asking where I come from. Seattle, I told her.

It was early November, and the trees had lost their fall colors. It was late in the year for a campsite to be open, and the place was nearly empty, the office full of kitschy gifts and dusty packages of snack foods.

We got to talking about bears in the nearby woods above the campground and dogs that might protect you from them, and somehow the conversation moved on to how, in times past, phones had dials, and there were party lines, and neighbors could spend the day listening in on each other's conversations. She relaxed a bit, and I thought I'd go back and visit with her after setting up my camp and having supper.

Take your pick of any site, she offered. I chose a spot by the creek, right next to an open field. A family of ducks swam noisily by, and over the field, the sunset lit up the clouds. I pulled out my one-burner butane stove and warmed up some soup.

A bit later, a beat-up RV pulled in, small compared to those I saw in the big RV parks, but much bigger than my tiny truck-camper. An elderly man got out. He said he was on his way to Colorado, and he hoped his RV would make it that far. It kept dying at stop signs, he explained. He thought maybe it had been sitting too long, and he commented, more to himself than to me, that he might try pouring some alcohol in the tank. Something about his old, worn rig made me think his trip to Colorado was more about a search for a home or a job than a vacation. I didn't get a chance to ask, though. The old man's son came blustering out of the store, yelling to his dad.

It was getting dark, and there was a bonfire outside the camp store, but no one pulled up a chair. I headed back to my camper, turned on the inside light, and closed the door. I spread out the bed, climbed in, and opened the door now and then to try to catch a glimpse of an owl or a moonrise.

WHITESBURG, KENTUCKY—To get to Whitesburg, Kentucky, you follow rivers through twisting valleys, climb over ridges, and pass through tiny hamlets where old wood-frame houses are crowded between steep hillsides and the highway. The entrance to Whitesburg is an abrupt turn off the main highway, then down a steep road, with a surprise appearance of brightly painted human-shaped sculptures along the road side. A right turn across a bridge, and past the new Kentucky Moonshine distillery, and you're at the big, wooden Appalshop building.

Appalshop was the reason I'd come to Whitesburg. This Appalachian cultural center houses a theater, a community radio station (WMMT), archives of films from decades of local filmmaking, and an art gallery. There I met Ada Smith, 28, daughter of two of the original founders of Appalshop. Smith is a slight woman with shoulder-length brown hair, oversized glasses, and a quiet voice revealing the light accent of a Kentucky native.

Whitesburg is lively compared to how it was, Smith told me. She was especially excited that the community had revoked its prohibition on liquor sales, and suddenly new nightspots were opening. Young people were returning. Old-time traditional music as well as punk and other genres were flowering,

Entering Whitesburg, Kentucky, you are greeted by these sculptures.

and that new distillery I passed on my way was a sign that local businesses can thrive here.

Smith ran me through the history of Appalshop. In 1969, during the War on Poverty, the federal Office of Economic Opportunity sent portable film cameras and editing gear out to a half dozen poor communities around the United States and held film workshops. Only two of those locations were rural; one of them was Whitesburg, Kentucky. The idea was to train young people to make films as a way to both improve their job prospects and tell their own stories, instead of being subjects in the stories outsiders wanted to tell.

The young people who showed up to do this work managed to continue creating films about their communities when the federal money dried up. Ada Smith's father, Henry Smith, was one of them. Henry Smith was one of eight children of a coal miner. Her mother, a filmmaker from Hazard, Kentucky, was also part of Appalshop's early staff.

"I got off the school bus right in front of this building," Ada told me.

What was it like to have Appalshop open in the midst of a quiet little coal town?

"Like a spaceship landed," she replied.

Appalachia is famously poor, something the rest of the country got wind of when a 1964 presidential commission assigned to investigate the area issued a report of impoverished coal-mining families that shocked the nation's conscience. The photos showed gaunt figures and malnourished children. Today, malnutrition remains a problem, but, ironically, it's coupled with obesity caused by a diet high in fat, salt, and calories yet lacking nutrients.

Appalachia is reeling from the loss of jobs as the coal industry winds down. Mountains have been blown apart for the last seams of coal, rivers and creeks have been filled in with mining debris, and coal ash wastewater lakes sit behind unmaintained dams, threatening communities below. Plus, black lung disease has made a comeback since it was nearly eradicated. This is the legacy of the coal industry, which local politicians still claim is a source of prosperity.

According to author and sociologist Cynthia M. Duncan, Appalachia had intentionally been kept isolated and controlled.

"Historians have shown that the large Northeastern utilities and Midwestern utilities were pitting one small company against another. In the face of this bitter competition, coal operators tried to control everything about workers' lives to keep their labor costs down," Duncan told reporters from the PBS

documentary series *Frontline*.[1] "And part of controlling everything was to not educate people, to be in control of the minis-
ters, the doctors, the stores . . . and to discourage workers' participation in community life, making the workers dependent
on the coal operators for everything about their livelihood and
their community."

Jobs in coal mining in Kentucky have fallen from 38,000 in
1983 to 17,000 30 years later, according to *The Washington Post*.[2]
But a sense persists that relying on others is shameful, and a
stoic self-reliance is a source of pride.

As an adolescent growing up in that environment, Ada
Smith was quite sure she wanted to leave. After high school,
she and a cousin took off for Seattle, which she thought was the
coolest. The city had a vibrant gay community, punk rock, and
protest.

But then she started to miss home. Her homesickness hit
abruptly as she was marching in a protest in Olympia, Washington, at the state capitol building, and someone began singing, "I
Hate the Capitalist System." She asked, but no one knew that it
was written just south of Smith's home in Harlan County, and
that the lyrics were written by a coal miner's wife who laments
her husband's tuberculosis and the loss of her child to starva-
tion during a terrible strike.

Smith attended Hampshire College in western Massachu-
setts, but there she found herself stereotyped by other students.
She had recently come out as queer, but based on her accent,
people assumed she was racist and homophobic.

She decided to go home. "I knew how messed up it was,"
she said. But "I wanted to give back to a place that gave so much
to me."

It was a lonely return. Most of the other young people she'd
known had left. She and other 20-somethings formed the STAY

project, a network of young Kentuckians "working to create, advocate for, and participate in safe, sustainable, engaging, and inclusive communities throughout Appalachia and beyond." The informal goal is to keep young people from leaving.

Smith followed in her parents' footsteps and began to take on leadership positions at Appalshop.

PINE MOUNTAIN, KENTUCKY—I asked Ada Smith where I might find a place to camp for the night, and she suggested calling Jim Webb, poet, WMMT radio DJ, and proprietor of Wiley's Last Resort, "the primitive campsite at the end of the whirled," according to its website. The resort is part of a nature preserve on top of Pine Mountain, the second-highest mountain in Kentucky. Wiley's was closed for the winter, but Webb invited me to come up anyway and gave me directions—follow the road that climbs straight up from Whitesburg, and at the top, take the second left. I made a wrong turn and wound up on a deeply rutted road, passing derelict Airstream trailers and abandoned cars before I realized my mistake. By the time I got turned around and made it to the resort, Webb, sporting a long, mountain-man white beard, and his partner, a pleasant woman with a gray bun, were outside, ready to head into town to run some errands. They showed me where I could camp, though, next to the small lake backed up behind the "We-giva Dam" and close to the "Eyeful Shower," which, sadly, was also closed for the season. Nearby, the roof of the former bathhouse has become the Sand Bar & Gorilla, an open-air venue for festivities of all sorts. The place had pink flamingoes, strings of lanterns, and memorabilia on all sides.

Webb traces his roots back to Daniel Boone and Pocahontas. His family owns some of the oldest log cabins in the region, a couple of which he has moved, log by log, onto the premises.

Wiley's Last Resort hosts the Mountain Justice Kentucky gatherings above the lake on a flattened section of the mountain where a quarry had been filled in. Stages, solar panels, and compost toilets make the site perfect for the summer gathering where activists and musicians play music and strategize for an end to mountaintop removal.

A post-coal economy?

"Where there once were water producing mountains—now there are barren scraped-biologically dead toxic wastelands," a statement on the Mountain Justice website reads. "Water is going to be more important to future generations than coal. You cannot drink coal."

With the decline in the coal industry, Smith and her friends think a lot about Appalachia's economic future. The old development strategies focused on serving the coal and gas industries, such as a proposed nitrous plant for creating fracking fluids. The coal and gas companies own a lot of land but pay few taxes, Smith said. And they have an outsized influence over the elite who control the local government.

Some public officials consider a new prison the answer. The Letcher County Planning Commission settled on a location for a new federal prison in the summer of 2015: the flattened site of a former mountaintop removal in Roxana, Kentucky. Initially, the Bureau of Prisons was reluctant because the site is so remote and building there would be expensive. But the district congressman, Representative Hal Rogers, took up the cause, and his position as chairman of the House Appropriations Committee gave him the clout to push through the project. The federal budget, signed into law by President Obama in

December 2015, included $450 million for the prison. Planning commission cochair Elwood Cornett was quoted in a local paper as saying, "The coal industry has laid off so many people and here's the prospect of not only jobs but economic impact from all the things going on."[3] Supporters say the prison will result in 300 to 400 permanent jobs, although critics point out that most of these jobs will go to outsiders. Sylvia Ryerson, a Letcher County resident and a journalist with Appalshop's radio station, WMMT 88.7, called for thinking creatively about job creation. Why not invest those hundreds of millions of federal dollars in a state-of-the-art drug rehabilitation center? she asked in an opinion column in *The Daily Yonder*. What if, instead of siting one new prison, the community focused its efforts on starting 35 locally owned companies, each employing 10 people? These are approaches that lead to a "restorative economy," she argued.[4]

"The region must seek more reliable options than prison building, especially in the midst of a nationwide push to reduce the prison population and address the failed mass-incarceration policies that drove the prison boom of the previous three decades," wrote Panagioti Tsolkas, the coordinator of the Human Rights Defense Center's Prison Ecology Project, in an opinion piece published by the *Lexington Herald-Leader*.[5]

Renewables may be part of the answer to replacing coal mining jobs. While the coal industry has been laying off workers, jobs in wind power production are up 16 percent, and jobs in the solar power industry rose 200 percent between 2011 and 2014.[6] According to the International Renewable Energy Agency (IRENA), renewable energy employment in the United States reached 724,000 jobs in 2014, a 16 percent increase from the previous year.[7]

Economic empowerment in Appalachia

Economic empowerment in Appalshop will need to go beyond renewable energy. Ada Smith is part of a team that is literally mapping the region's assets, identifying what people here have to build on: natural resources, Appalachian culture, and local business and talent. The team uses theater to help elicit residents' visions of the future and story circles to produce plays based on their own experiences. The work is very political, Smith noted. People worry that suggesting a future beyond existing industries (such as coal) might be threatening to those industries.

Still, alternatives to the coal and prison industries are starting to emerge. Small-scale agriculture is one such option. Grow Appalachia, based at Berea College, makes small grants throughout the region to help people grow and preserve their own food. The organization partners with local groups to supply seeds and organic soil amendments, and it provides know-how on planning a garden, cooking heart-healthy meals, and preserving food.

Grow Appalachia also looks for opportunities to build the next level of the food economy; it offers small grants for hoop houses or other means to expand the growing season or to turn surplus harvests into products to sell.

Jane Jacobs's "import substitution" is an economic development strategy that seems especially relevant here. Produce the food yourself—to consume, share, or sell—instead of buying from outside the region, and you create opportunities for entrepreneurs and jobs.

Import substitution takes on an additional dimension when people replace imported processed, fatty, nutrient-poor foods with fresh local greens, beans, and tomatoes. Kentucky's obesity rate is above 30 percent, up from around 12 percent in 1990, according to state statistics.[8] Promoting healthy food can save the region the hardship and expense of obesity-related chronic disease while increasing the area's quality of life.

Culture: another import substitution

Locally produced music, theater, and visual art are also forms of import substitution. Turn off the mass-produced stuff—the Hollywood movies, the commercial music—support local musicians at locally owned venues, and you help build the local economy. More money circulates locally. People patronize independent businesses instead of shopping at Walmart or eating at McDonald's. Local musicians and restaurant owners and staff most likely spend at least some of their earnings locally as well. Every transaction that keeps money local means one more neighbor is getting paid, while almost all the money spent at corporate-owned chains quickly leaves the community. So Appalshop's focus on theater, art, filmmaking, and radio station not only rebuilds the local culture, it also helps develop the local economy.

I was the only one in the audience at an old-time music jam that took place at Appalshop, but that was because everyone else brought an instrument. A group of men and women played fiddles, guitars, and mandolins onstage. One would play an opening bar of a favorite, such as "Angeline the Baker," and the rest of the musicians would quickly join in, faces stoical, toes tapping. In between songs, they'd catch up on local happenings.

In the lobby, recent works by a local artist were on display, and refreshments were available. Suspended from the walls were handmade quilts, one with "Appalshop" appliquéd on a rendition of hills, valleys, and a clear, blue river running down the center.

Could Whitesburg become the Nashville or New Orleans of Appalachia? Smith was only half joking when she suggested it. Now that alcohol is legal, nightspots are flourishing. Whitesburg now boasts two live music venues, a locally owned tattoo parlor, the newly opened distillery, and several restaurants. Culture isn't merely substituting for imports, it's creating an "export." Or, at least, it's attracting folks from outside who spend their money in the town, which amounts to the same thing.

Discussion of economic development often leaves out the ways in which a local economy is embedded within a community. Local culture and local food bring people together; music venues, farmers' markets, and quilting bees create gathering spaces. Delineating the "economy" as something apart from community and culture becomes impossible. Is a farmers' market mainly an economic institution because money changes hands? Or is it a music venue? Or a place to catch up on news and to exchange ideas on politics? Or a place to check out possible romantic partners? In societies throughout the world, locally rooted markets serve in all of these ways.

Appalachian voices and culture

The cultural resurgence Appalshop promotes, according to Alexander Gibson, Appalshop's new executive director, helps people find their voices.

I met Gibson in his small office at the organization's headquarters. Gibson, 30, joined the staff at Appalshop in 2015. He has café-au-lait skin and a short beard and identifies himself as mixed race. Born in a black neighborhood in Cincinnati, he moved to Jackson County, Kentucky, to a town that was essentially made up of his extended family. Both his parents died, and he wound up attending boarding school and later college, graduating from the University of Pennsylvania with a law degree with an emphasis in business. He clerked for a federal judge, studied in London and Thailand, and practiced corporate law in Philadelphia and Louisville.

"Most people who grow up in this area are touched by some sort of serious and debilitating poverty," he told me. "Until the point where I got my first six-figure salary, I wanted nothing more than to leave Kentucky."

His work with bank and corporate clients, while successful and lucrative, left him unsatisfied. "I can win a case, and that feels good on a certain level," he said. "But for what end?"

Boredom with "corporate life, bourbon sipping, cocktail party schmoozing," mixed with a longing for his rural upbringing, mountains, and hills made him consider returning to his roots. So when Ada Smith called, asking him to apply for a position at Appalshop, he had to think about it.

"How do you make your life matter? What can you touch, what can you do, to be important?" Enabling Appalachians to tell their own story is important, he says.

Gibson has faced real challenges in returning to rural eastern Kentucky. "There's a lot of racism," he replied when I asked him what his life was like. "It's what you would expect. It has been awful.

"The relationship of my color to this region shapes every social interaction, every decision I make, every shop I go into, every person I talk to—it's on my mind almost every moment."

Nonetheless, as director of Appalshop, he keeps his focus on the experience of all Appalachians. The ridicule and disparagement directed at them from mainstream media, for example, is something he thinks about often. "You can make jokes about Appalachians," he said. "They're barefoot, hillbillies, no teeth. They don't have toilets. That's funny to people? That's not a tragedy we have to solve?

"I don't know why that's funny," he continued. "We can't talk about black people that way.

"People grow up seeing themselves depicted on television as the *Beverly Hillbillies* or the *Simpsons*," he said. "Many just want to leave. There's a lot of self-hate in the region."

This scorn for Appalachian people expressed outside the region makes it all the more important that they have a voice— that they define their place and their culture on their own terms.

"If you don't have that voice, or agency, your story becomes hostage to the teller," Gibson said. Conservative radio, then, can convince people that "Obama and the EPA are taking away your job.

"Art can create the same sense of agency, engagement, and self-determination as owning a business," he said. "There is a self-actualizing process. Someone can make a film or see themselves in a film or see their issue in a film."

It may not be part of Appalshop's strategic plan, but this African American leader's defense of the dignity of the predominantly white residents of eastern Kentucky is powerful, and it challenges stereotypes about both black and white in this region.

Another way Appalshop challenges stereotypes is via its radio station, WMMT, which for years has been the voice of "mountain people's music, culture, and social issues." Local DJs play not only gospel, old-time music, and bluegrass but also contemporary music and hip-hop.

The station's programming recognizes the diverse communities that make up Appalachia, including the thousands of residents who are inmates at the seven state and federal penitentiaries plus those in the regional jails and detention facilities that fall within WMMT's listening area. Many inmates are incarcerated far from home, brought to the mountains from distant cities, and they tune in to the 7 p.m. Monday night show, *Hip-Hop from the Hill Top*. Letters from inmates are full of praise for this program and the DJs.

One night, a listener called in to ask the station to convey a message to one of the prison inmates, since reaching an inmate by telephone can be difficult and expensive. The DJ for that night's *Hip-Hop from the Hill Top* agreed, and a new project was born. Every Monday from 7 to 9 p.m., family and friends of inmates at the various prisons call in to the radio show and record greetings, family news, and messages of love and encouragement. Then from 9 to 10 p.m., the radio station broadcasts an uninterrupted stream of those recorded messages.

"I haven't forgotten you. I hope you are well and staying focused," said one of the women who called in. I listened to the live stream of the show after I returned home, and I heard dozens of messages in this vein. "I just wanted to give you a shout-out tonight. I love you, and I think about you all the time."

Ada Smith is one of the DJs. "People asked us why we would broadcast these messages," remarked Smith, whose on-air handle is DJ Jewelz.

It's an interesting question for a mostly white community about a program that serves a mainly nonwhite prison population. Smith believes it matters that her neighbors in Kentucky better understand the lives and families of the black and brown inmates who are imprisoned in their midst, and perhaps hearing these words of love will open minds and hearts.

In any case, this predominantly white organization has

taken a stand, in effect declaring that the black and brown people who live among them, even if they are incarcerated, are also part of the community, and their experience, and the voices of their friends and family, matter.

Combatting despair, building dignity

On my last night in Whitesburg, I sat at the new music hot spot, Summit City Lounge, with Ada Smith while the evening's band set up.

Summit City is located in a historic building that once held the town's general store. The bands performing here range from Lee Bains III and the Glory Fires, an Alabama rock band that "ponders Southern identity in a welter of cranked-up guitars, bristling drums, and rasping, hollering vocals," to Company of Thieves, a Chicago-based indie band. Summit City is committed to community-centered, locally owned businesses; to local food when possible; to small breweries and distilleries; and to mountain art and music and to bringing people together.

Job scarcity is especially tough on the young guys, Smith told me. Many have experienced violence, often at the hands of their dads. They don't know what it means to do well now that the coal jobs are gone, so they have trouble figuring out their identity.

The despair in this region plays a part in setting the tone for the whole country. Anger grows out of this despair, as people feel left out or pushed aside—and the projection of that anger onto people of color, environmentalists, immigrants, and others whom right-wing shock jocks blame helps fuel support for right-wing politics.

A culture rooted in authentic self-respect and a secure, locally embedded economy offers a more stable foundation. From

that foundation, fear and intolerance can give way to understanding.

When I met him in Berea, Kentucky, David Cooke of Grow
Appalachia told me about the grandmothers and grandfathers
who had always grown food and preserved it to get through
the winter. The tradition was lost when so many were occupied
with coal mining jobs, he said. But now, the next generation
wants to be more self-reliant. Growing and preserving food
contributes to that self-reliance, and the abundance of food-
stuff also creates new reasons for exchange. The forms vary—
some give away their extra zucchini to friends and family who
later bring by apple pie. Others earn cash at farm stands and
farmers' markets, or by selling to local restaurants, schools, or
stores. This exchange spreads wealth and reconnects people.
Gifts of food within a community, like other gifts, tend to be
reciprocated. Whether or not money changes hands, an economy becomes more active and meets more people's needs.

In this respect, the people of Appalachia might be ahead of
the rest of the country. This region already has long-standing
traditions of making do, of creating beautiful quilts pieced together from discarded clothes and bedsheets, of teaching and
learning music on front porches and coming together for open
mics and square dances, and of growing and preserving food.
The new leaders at Appalshop are working together to reconnect this culture, strengthening a local identity that can be free
of domination by coal corporations and the prison-industrial
complex and expanding it to include the full diversity of their
communities.

Greensboro's Battle over Story

On February 1, 1960, four African American students sat down at a Woolworths lunch counter in Greensboro, North Carolina, and asked for service. They didn't get their coffee or a menu, or a polite word, but the next day they returned, along with more than a dozen others. And the day after that.

Some of the older residents, black and white, warned them against stirring things up. But the students didn't quit even when whites threw coffee or catsup on them. Gradually, more and more supporters joined in, filling the store and the streets outside, people everywhere began boycotting Woolworths stores, sales dropped dramatically, and the owner gave in and began offering service to all comers.

One of the first things I did when I got to Greensboro was to visit that lunch counter, where the shop floor, walls, counters, and stools are preserved as they were during that famous sit-in. The store is now part of the International Civil Rights Center and Museum, which opened on February 1, 2010, 50 years to the day after the first sit-in.

In the museum's lower floors, displays offer context to the lives of the protesters and their families. I walked with other visitors through the "Hall of Shame" exhibits showing the lynchings and firebombings that terrorized African American communities during the hundred-plus years after slavery ended.

One small detail particularly caught my eye, chilling because of how ordinary it was: a Jim Crow–era guidebook that lists the places black travelers could safely stop for food, gas, or a bed for the night. The information in the booklet could make the difference between surviving a trip through the South or not.

The museum shows how the terrorizing of African American families held society in the grip of white supremacy. While the form changes, the race-based violence and exclusion continue.

Even opening the museum was a major struggle. In 1993, the Woolworths Corporation closed the store with the lunch counter and announced plans to demolish the building. It took local activists 17 years to secure the building, raise the money for renovation, and open the doors of the museum. Voters in Greensboro twice rejected bond measures to help cover the cost.

"This museum exists because there was a time that we don't want to go back to," Franklin McCain, one of the original sit-in participants, told National Public Radio. "It also represents a kind of beacon for what's possible, and it says to people that all sorts of good things are possible if people work together and respect each other."

I had come to Greensboro to learn about race and the battle over the story of race in America. We had just finished a special issue of *YES! Magazine*, entitled "Making It Right," that explored what it would take to finally get to the root of persistent racial violence and exclusion in American society. Policies and elections, as important as they are, aren't enough. The work we need to do involves shifting beliefs, changing institutions and obsolete habits, and, for white people, giving up our privilege. That sort of cultural work happens most powerfully in communities, in the places where we live, work, worship, debate, and raise our children. At least that was what I had come to believe.

I chose to visit Greensboro both because of its civil rights history and because the citizens of Greensboro embarked on a controversial Truth and Reconciliation Commission process to deal with a deadly racially charged incident from its recent past.

The Truth and Reconciliation Commission (TRC) process has been practiced for decades, and it was most fully developed in South Africa after the fall of apartheid. The commission there was charged with hearing the stories of victims of apartheid and also those of the perpetrators; in some cases, it offered amnesty. According to reports, the nation was riveted by the hearings. Fania Davis, a prominent U.S. advocate of the TRC process, wrote in *YES! Magazine* that it "established a spirit of forgiveness that helped the country transcend hundreds of years of hatred and violence and liberated millions of Africans from the yoke of apartheid."[1] I had worked with Davis on her piece calling for a Truth and Reconciliation Commission process in the United States. So I wanted to see how it had worked in Greensboro.

The massacre

On November 3, 1979, Ku Klux Klansmen and American Nazi Party members shot at a group of protesters organized by the Communist Workers Party in a black neighborhood in Greensboro, killing five protesters and wounding nine. One member of the Klan was also wounded.

The Truth and Reconciliation Commission in Greensboro was called to review these events and their immediate aftermath.

"I got there while there were still people on the ground and being taken away by ambulances," Joyce Hobson-Johnson told me. She and her husband, Reverend Nelson Johnson, had helped organize the march for workers' justice and civil rights that had been hit by the attack. I caught up with her after a community activity at her church and asked her about her recollections.

"I was desperately searching for our two children, who were seven and eight years old," she said. "My husband had not only been stabbed by a Nazi, but was dragged by the police

Joyce Hobson-Johnson was a witness to the massacre and one of those who advocated for a Truth and Reconciliation Commission in Greensboro.

and arrested." Hobson-Johnson is a small, middle-aged African American woman, who chose her words carefully as she answered my questions.

The police had been notified that a march would be taking place, and a Klan member, who was also a police informant, told them that the Klan planned a violent attack. Still, the police chose to stay away until after the shootings. It turned out that the police informant was actually a key organizer of the attack.

All of these facts were established during the trials. And television news cameras, on site to record the protest, captured video of the shootings. Still, two criminal trials ended with acquittals for the white-supremacist shooters by all-white juries. A later civil trial held the shooters, the police, and the Klan jointly liable for one death.

I met Joyce Hobson-Johnson at the Beloved Community Center, which shares a brick two-story building with the Faith Community Church near downtown Greensboro. The name comes from Martin Luther King Jr.'s vision of relationships that "realize the equality, dignity, worth, and potential of every person," according to the center's website.

Reverend Nelson Johnson, Hobson-Johnson's husband and a cofounder and executive director of the Beloved Community Center, is also a pastor at the Faith Community Church. Hobson-Johnson, who has been a civil rights activist since the 1960s, currently serves on the North Carolina NAACP State Executive Board.

"Those of us who were spared our lives were maligned for years," she replied when I asked her about the aftermath of the shootings. "People were too afraid to continue the organizing." And the community was polarized, unsure how to interpret the event. Some wanted to call it a shoot-out; others termed it a massacre.

A Truth and Reconciliation Commission

In 2004, 25 years after the shootings took place, Hobson-Johnson, Johnson, and other Greensboro citizens formed a Truth and Reconciliation Commission to get to the bottom of what had happened and who was involved, and, they hoped, to begin the healing.

The move was controversial. The Greensboro City Council voted, along race lines, not to participate, and many residents, black and white, opposed holding the hearings, believing they would stir up old wounds and anger. Without official sanction, the commission had no power to subpoena witnesses. Nonetheless, a group of citizens convened, held hearings, interviewed hundreds of residents, and issued their findings in May 2006.

Still, the controversy over the commission findings was almost as great as the controversy over the massacre itself. According to Jill E. Williams, executive director of the commission, some residents, especially white residents, had hoped the commission would bring about increased trust and even forgiveness. "Although there were a few notable moments during the truth process in which apologies and forgiveness were offered, this group tends to assume that Greensboro's truth and reconciliation process was not successful," she wrote in a 2009 report on the commission.[2]

Others were more interested in institutional reform, according to Williams. The commission recommended, for example, establishing a police citizens' review board.

The commission's clearest outcome may be that it helped end what Ed Whitfield describes as "a kind of he-said-she-said argument." Whitfield, a prominent African American activist and comanaging director of the Fund for Democratic Communities, was one of the group of community leaders who helped establish the Truth and Reconciliation Commission. The commission's report is the most thorough narrative of "what really happened, and how it happened, and what difference it made," he told me.

"Most local media outlets report the facts more accurately now than they did prior to the report's release," Williams wrote. "Similarly, Greensboro residents, as evidenced in part in local blogs, discuss the 1979 events with a more accurate understanding of the facts."

Michael Ignatieff, who reported on the Truth and Reconciliation Commission in South Africa, put it this way: truth commissions "reduce the number of lies that can be circulated unchallenged in public discourse."[3]

In the summer of 2015, community leaders placed a plaque marking the location where the shootings occurred. I went to see it with my host in Greensboro, James Lamar Gibson, a 20-something African American activist and an early volunteer for the commission. He and his Haitian American partner, Roodline Volcy, offered me the use of their spare bedroom in the duplex they share with their dog.

The word "massacre" appears on the marker, Gibson pointed out—an important step toward laying to rest the phony "shoot-out" narrative that had been used to excuse the shootings. That marker is one outcome of the TRC process.

I happened to be in Greensboro on the thirty-sixth anniversary of the shootings, and Gibson and I attended the commemoration at the Maplewood Cemetery marking the event, standing with a handful of others as the November sky darkened and the group read out loud the names of the people who had died.

In any community, big events, such as a massacre, have effects that continue to ripple out. The same is true of an intervention, like the TRC process. Two researchers, Mary Louise Frampton, a law professor at Berkeley, and David Anderson Hooker, now a professor of conflict transformation and peace building at Notre Dame, conducted hundreds of interviews in Greensboro to determine how the public viewed the commission's work. What they learned, according to Gibson, is that many people didn't want to focus on the massacre, which they find traumatizing or embarrassing, but they do want to address the core issues of race and inequity, and their impacts on policing, housing, and education.

Counter Stories

For the last year, a group of 15 to 20 people have been meeting as part of the Counter Stories Project to organize "restorative" conversations. The name references both the original lunch counter sit-ins and the need to "counter" the contentious narratives that still divide Greensboro residents.

"We've been stuck in an old conversation for a couple of decades now," Gibson said. "We want to have an army of people with restorative conversation skills, so we can get past the divisiveness and imagine together a different sort of Greensboro."

They began with facilitators' trainings and then developed story circles, in which police officers and other residents were able to have the difficult discussions about police-community encounters that don't ordinarily take place. There have been two rounds of each so far, according to Gibson, who is one of the core organizers. The local alternative weeklies have covered the conversations, which involved groups ranging from churches and social agencies to the police force and city council. And, as with the original TRC process, there has been plenty of controversy. Still, trained facilitators now help bring a skillful anti-racist voice into community conversations and broaden the imagination about what's possible, Gibson said.

Beloved community

There is discord over police-community relations all over the United States. But is combatting racism place-based work?

"You have to bring it home," Hobson-Johnson said when I asked her this question. "Ultimately, we have to fight racism, economic disparity, health disparities, education disparities, all those things at home because that's where we live."

Hobson-Johnson acknowledged that combatting injustice at the state and national levels is also important—she is deeply engaged with her work on the statewide NAACP Executive Council.

"But to really make a difference, you have to have relationships and build a new culture of possibility, what we call beloved community.

"We've met with some of the Klan and Nazis," Hobson-Johnson told me. "They, too, struggle for their livelihoods and unfortunately have bought in to the lie that black people, Jewish people, gay people, immigrants are the problem, as opposed to the system."

It takes courage to meet with people who advocate racist violence. And it also takes courage to bring neighbors together to talk about race. But that's part of the process, she said, "even if it sometimes means we have to pull each other kicking and screaming together. When we get together, more and more we realize, hmmm, it's not so bad. . . .

"I don't mean everybody's gonna be hugging and kissing,"

she added, smiling. "But you respect and honor their dignity and worth, the equality of every person. That's something that is in itself revolutionary."

I was moved by her willingness to continue year after year reaching out to people who have advocated violence and brutality toward her community. And I was surprised again when Hobson-Johnson expanded her definition of those deserving respect to include nonhuman life: "the environment, the Earth, all of what's here," she said. "You can do that in place."

Renaissance Cooperative

Greensboro, like the rest of the country, has a long ways to go to put racism behind it. The poverty rate is more than three times higher among African Americans than among whites, for example.[4]

As I found often on this trip, in communities, people understand that the issues overlap. Gibson took me to see an old grocery store building that has been vacant for 18 years and will soon house a new food cooperative. Fresh, healthy food will be available to a predominantly African American neighborhood that "has been left out for years and is sick of being left out," Gibson said. "In the past, the government talked about addressing blight, but they didn't invest—in fact, they disinvested. The co-op came out of the sense that we needed to do something to address this for ourselves."

To make clear that the co-op is truly community owned, everyone who joins is called an "owner" rather than a member, he told me.

"For years, we wanted to create an ownership culture," said Ed Whitfield, an organizer of both the Truth and Reconciliation Commission and the co-op.

"This is not a radical neighborhood or community," Whitfield said. "A lot of folks are just trying to make ends meet, to succeed individually. The idea that people can do something together if they pool their resources, draw on sufficient amounts of support, and maintain the onus—this is a new idea that people are getting to like."

"It's huge," said Gibson. "There's new energy. Now everyone is thinking about what we are going to build next."

Greensboro has many unresolved issues. Still, this community evolved from one where a KKK shooting took place with the complicity of police to one where police and community members sit together in circles. African Americans, who were excluded from the simplest participation in community life, like sitting at a lunch counter, now own their own lunch spot—and the grocery store that comes with it. The change seems slow, but perhaps the tough truth telling, the persistent search for reconciliation, and the new community ownership culture are shifting Greensboro's sense of itself. The system of white supremacy is powerful, but so is the vision of a beloved community.

My next stop was Harrisonburg, Virginia, a national center of restorative justice. I also planned to visit Newark, New Jersey, where a newly elected African American mayor is working to revitalize the city in a way that will benefit, not displace, communities of color; and Ithaca, New York, where a theater ensemble is using community-based storytelling and plays to open up conversations about race in a predominantly white college town.

Restorative Justice and the Harrisonburg Police

HARRISONBURG, VIRGINIA — Restorative justice (RJ), which has roots in indigenous circle processes, is a way of dealing with conflict and violations of trust. The practice is designed to restore relationships broken by a crime or other discord. In classic cases, a victim of a crime and the offender meet in a circle with others who have a stake in the outcome—the victim gets to ask questions about the crime, the perpetrator offers an apology and may add context to the event, and together they work out terms of reparations. Advocates say this approach, compared to that of the criminal justice system, is more likely to result in healing for the victim, real accountability from the offender, and a less divided community.

I came to Harrisonburg, Virginia, to learn about a practice that is spreading across the country as a substitute for approaches based on punishment and prison time. The criminal justice system disproportionately punishes people of color, from traffic stops through sentencing and on through post-prison employment. The United States has more than 2 million people behind bars, the highest number and the highest rate of incarceration in the world; this country imprisons its public at three and a half times the rate of Europe. Furthermore, although people of color make up 30 percent of the U.S. population, they account for 60 percent of the prison population; one in three black men can expect to spend time in prison over the course of their lifetimes.[1] And once convicted, anyone finds it harder to get a job, housing, credit, or social services. So diverting people from the criminal justice system, especially young people, is one piece of untangling institutionalized racism.

"I think restorative justice offers a shift in the way we view people, from seeing them as objects to viewing people as human beings," Jodie Geddes, a 20-something African American woman, told me when I met her at a coffee shop at Eastern Mennonite University (EMU). Geddes is a graduate student in the university's Conflict Transformation and Peacebuilding program and also had interned with the Harrisonburg Police Department.

Jodie Geddes, a student of restorative justice at Eastern Mennonite University.

"If we treat people as human beings, we begin to ask, what is their story, and how does it contribute to the acts that they've committed?" said Geddes. "The police and the system of policing begin to recognize the other parts of my story that may have led me there."

I was staying in an apartment adjacent to the EMU campus that I'd rented from a friend of a friend. I explored Harrisonburg and caught up on writing and emails in between learning all I could about restorative justice as practiced in this small city in Virginia's Shenandoah Valley.

An ethos of listening and respect, of peacemaking built on truth telling, could infuse the culture of Harrisonburg, noted Dr. Carl Stauffer, codirector of the Zehr Institute for Restorative Justice, a spin-off of EMU that works to fuse RJ approaches into other facets of society beyond the criminal justice system. Projects based in Harrisonburg include Come to the Table, a project that explores and seeks to heal family and community legacies of racism, going as far back as the time of slavery. Among those involved are descendants of slave owners and slave traders, who recognize that their families' wealth is a direct result of wealth extracted from the forced labor of enslaved people.[2]

Other schools in Harrisonburg are also involved in RJ efforts. James Madison University now incorporates restorative justice into its responses to student discipline and conflict via its Office of Student Accountability and Restorative Practices.

Younger students, too, are learning about restorative justice. I visited a Harrisonburg middle school and sat with a group of sixth-graders who had chosen to sit in a circle during recess, taking turns to speak one at a time on the same topic, and listening intently to whoever held the talking piece that gives that person sole permission to speak. They spoke about what it means to be heard, and what it means to really listen to their classmates and to feel empathy. On other occasions, their teacher told me, their talking circles center on more specific concerns—for example, disagreements among students.

The sixth-grade girls represented a wide range of ethnic backgrounds. Harrisonburg is a refugee resettlement area, and many of the students had only recently arrived from conflict zones. The girls said they felt empowered by being heard during the circle, knowing that they could have their say without being criticized or interrupted.

Their teacher, trained in RJ techniques, is experimenting with how to bring that sense of trust and confidence into her classroom. Posted on one wall is a Mayan credo, quoted by poet Luis Valdez and adapted for classroom use by educator Curtis Acosta.

In Lak 'ech

Tú eres mi otro yo.	You are my other me.
Si te hago daño a ti,	If I do harm to you,
Me hago daño a mi mismo.	I do harm to myself.
Si te amo y respeto,	If I love and respect you,
Me amo y respeto yo.	I love and respect myself.

Restorative justice is making inroads into schools of all levels in Harrisonburg. But could it become part of the culture beyond the classroom?

Kathy Evans, an assistant professor of education at EMU, introduced me to Police Lieutenant Kurt Boshart, who is striving to bring restorative justice into police work. We met at Bowl of Good, a quirky restaurant near EMU that sells meals by the bowl. Boshart is tall, with close-cropped hair, and he came to the café wearing civilian clothes.

"Law enforcement is not as readily accepted within the community as it once was," Boshart said as he explained a source of his interest in restorative justice.

Dr. Carl Stauffer, codirector of the Zehr Institute for Restorative
Justice (left), and Harrisonburg Police Lieutenant Kurt Boshart (right).

Legitimacy matters to police departments. "Goals—such
as high success rates for investigating crimes and preventing
crime—depend on the willingness of the public to cooperate
with police, to provide information to the police, and to will-
ingly obey the law, all of which can be affected by the department's reputation for legitimacy," according to a report by the
Police Executive Research Forum.[3]

Part of the solution to police-community conflict is "procedural justice," the way police officers treat people during everyday interactions on the streets, Boshart said. He is urging police
officers to listen more, to show more respect to the people they
stop. "It's really about teaching officers to give them a voice, to
allow them to talk and to not be judgmental."

But at a time when videos of black people beaten and shot
by police have become commonplace, much more is needed.

"Police are called during the worst of times, so everyone is
seeing each other during their worst moments, and that's the
basis of their relationship," Boshart noted. "The officer shows
up, and it's an adversarial situation, and that's how they leave—
adversarial."

What if instead "we could actually see each other for who we are?" Boshart said. And, although it took a long time to get to this point in our conversation, Boshart agreed that racial bias is a central challenge.

Boshart said that he urges rookie police officers to recognize that they have biases, and to avoid allowing those biases to dictate their responses to perceived threats. Boshart's example from a training he does with new officers uses his own experience to convey his point, as he explained:

> I'm white, I was brought up in a white neighborhood, I went to an all-white church, I went to an all-white school. Everything around my life was white. What I watched on the news is murders, robberies in the inner cities happening by African Americans. I listen to friends and family members who say, "You need to be careful of those people. You need to be careful because they're dangerous, they'll commit crimes." So I am painted a picture of this monster.

The moment took my breath away, not because it's news— we can surmise that many white officers have only encountered African Americans in conflict situations, and that their biases are lighting up as they make the split-second decision about whether to pull the trigger. Still, I was stunned by what followed:

> So if I'm faced, I have a white guy and an African American staring at me, saying, "I'm going to kill you," I'm more likely to shoot the African American because of this. I'm not saying that it's right, I'm not saying that my threat level wasn't the same. My perception of threat level is based off of that. Does that make sense? It doesn't make it any less real for

me as a person, for me as an officer. I still felt that my life was in danger. So that's where this controversy takes place nationwide.

"How do we change that?" Boshart asked. This question, which I believe was sincere, might be the most important one in American policing today.

What's needed, Boshart said, is anti-bias training. Plus, Boshart believes, police officers must come together with people of color in the community where they can get to know one another outside of a traffic stop or a crime scene.

"Sitting in a circle, where it's not adversarial, seeing the vulnerability of another person, goes a long way to building empathy. And the next time that officer sees that person on the street, he's now remembering that they had a conversation."

Could restorative justice—and the habits of respect and listening—shift the culture in Harrisonburg? Could it change the attitude of police and reduce the bias that has had such deadly consequences for brown and black people? Can the empathy evoked when people sit in a circle together as equals actually change things?

Like most of the United States, Harrisonburg still needs to do some tough truth telling about racism and trauma, and restorative justice doesn't replace that. Still, Harrisonburg educators are teaching members of the next generation to use tools that resolve conflict and evoke empathy, and at least some members of the police force are working to adopt these practices. Harrisonburg could become a city where a critical mass of people know when and how to use restorative circles to resolve conflicts, Stauffer believes. "We want people to hear and feel RJ in a whole bunch of different places so it feels commonplace."

Newark and the People Who Love It

It's a startling sight on a busy street in a run-down neighborhood of Newark, New Jersey. On a five-story brick building, windows partially boarded up, is a larger-than-life-size painting of a young girl, her black hair tied up in two high ponytails, her hands holding a mound of soil out of which grows the word "love." And she has sprouted two giant golden-orange butterfly wings.

Nearby, on a one-story wood-sided wall, giant portraits of Black Power leader Malcolm X and poet and Newark native son Amiri Baraka look over at a young man, who is staring straight out of the painting. The young man represents the artist, who is feeling the weight—and the inspiration—of carrying on the legacy of these heroes, according to my guide, Keith Aziz Hamilton.

On the November 2015 day of my visit, these murals were brand-new, among the 15 that were in the works or completed since Ras Baraka became mayor of Newark in 2014, and Hamilton was in charge of commissioning them. Hamilton, a former schoolteacher and a longtime friend of Mayor Baraka, is currently the manager of city-owned property. He has the warmth and toughness of a lifelong Newark resident and an infectious appreciation for the murals' artists.

"We wanted the murals to reflect family, peace in our neighborhood, love for yourself, and love for your neighborhood," Hamilton said. "And we wanted them to reflect beauty, some history, the place where you live."

Newark could use some beauty. It is rated one of the ten most dangerous cities in the country, and 28 percent of the population live below the poverty line.[1] Like many other U.S. cities, it has large areas of blight and entrenched, multigenerational poverty. But Newark is also the home of both the third-largest seaport in the United States and a major international airport, and it is located a mere 20-minute train ride from Manhattan. The city has a lot going for it.

Detail from a mural in Newark, New Jersey.

Mayor Ras Baraka began running for mayor 20 years ago, when he was just 24 years old. He is the son of the famous poet and playwright Amiri Baraka, and there are stories of Nina Simone and other cultural icons gathering at the family home. A group of Ras Baraka's friends and collaborators who grew up influenced by the older Baraka have been activists in the city for most of their lives. Hamilton, who was Baraka's campaign manager, is one of them.

For most of my road trip, I had focused on grassroots work, not elected officials. In Newark, though, I was interested in this new administration that had come directly out of neighborhood organizing and now was working at City Hall to end violence and lift up the prospects for the city's poor. Ras Baraka was the principal of Central High School in Newark and served on the municipal council before winning election as mayor and being sworn into office in 2014.

When Baraka took office, one of his first steps was to launch a Model Neighborhoods Initiative targeted at Clinton Hill in the South Ward and the Lower West Ward, two areas known for blight and poverty. The plan was to focus city, nonprofit, and residents' resources on cleanup, crime reduction, and housing, and to encourage businesses and artists in these two districts.

"It's a place-based strategy to pump a lot of resources into neighborhoods with significant blight and problems with crime—areas that have been neglected for years and years," Hamilton said.

Hamilton took me to visit the target neighborhoods; both are predominantly African American, with busy streets, vacant lots surrounded by chain-link fences, and buildings with boarded-up windows. Both also have well-maintained homes, parks, churches, and a smattering of businesses. In these neigh-

Keith Aziz Hamilton, head of Newark's city-owned property and the force behind the murals in Newark, New Jersey.

borhoods, murals have been popping up like flowers after a spring rain.

Progress here extends beyond murals. Mayor Baraka brings his own vision to the work of rebuilding this troubled city. He is committed to reducing violent crime, especially the murder rate. A video circulating on the Internet shows Baraka giving an impassioned speech at a rally that comes back over and over to "Round their asses up!" In the video, Baraka calls on the community to get involved—to get to know neighbors and to not tolerate violence in their homes and neighborhoods.

It might sound like a typical get-tough-on-crime stance, but Baraka favors a holistic approach to crime reduction; his administration is working to create jobs and recreational opportunities. Project Hope, for example, is hiring young people who were involved in violent crime and gang activities to help with reconstruction in the two target neighborhoods. Those who complete the program, which also includes regular check-ins with social services, receive free vocational training in one of three areas in which jobs are available: construction, automotive repair, and commercial driving. The city also works to find jobs and housing for ex-inmates during the critical time when they are returning to the community.

Economic development overall is a central priority of the Baraka administration. When I finally met the mayor himself, on a quick return visit to Newark in 2016, he told me he was proud that the city had reduced unemployment rates, although not as much as he wanted. He has announced a 15-dollar minimum wage for city workers to take effect by 2018. He has instituted a municipal I.D. system for immigrants that allows them to come at least partway out of the shadow. And the city is investing in new and refurbished housing.

The Baraka administration also supports the arts. Hamilton took me to see a massive bank building, the former Clinton Avenue Trust, with stately columns and an impressive facade, which stood abandoned and decaying for decades. The mayor and other city officials broke ground on the restoration of the building earlier that month; it will become affordable living and working spaces for local artists, and it will be renamed the Nina Simone House. In addition, the city is building an outdoor stage on the street to attract cultural events to the center of one of the mayor's two model neighborhoods, along with businesses.

"Trying to get financial institutions to invest at the level we need them to invest is the difficult part," Baraka told me. These neighborhoods have been disinvested in for the last 50 to 60 years, he said. Most of the new investment in the model neighborhoods is city money, "but we're not going to get to where we need it to be with just the city's push."

Hamilton and I stopped at one mural on the side of a furniture and appliance store that I now think of first when I think of Newark's murals. The store owner wanted to continue using the top strip of the long wall to advertise his mattresses, box springs, appliances, and floor samples. The artist, confined to painting the lower area along the sidewalk, spent a lot of time talking to passers-by, according to Hamilton. His work incorporated the art already there—the graffiti of previous artists. And he incorporated comments people made during those sidewalk conversations.

One sentence on the wall stood out, even though it was a small part of the long mural: "We the People LOVE this place." Nearby was the statement "In fact, we the people call this place our home."

Those phrases sum up some of the most important things I had learned on my travels. "We the People," the first phrase in the U.S. Constitution, speaks of us as powerful citizens—subjects, not objects—sovereigns of the place we call home.

"Love" reminds us that there are many dimensions of our relationship with place: the physical location, a network of relationships that add richness and complexity to daily life, and the intersecting cultures that create beauty and meaning. And

Wall paintings in Newark.

we share our place with other species who also make that place home. Each place has a history, told and untold, of all those who have lived there before, and each has possibilities we can't begin to imagine for the coming generations.

We the People LOVE this place: the artist made "love" the largest word. Love includes a commitment to the well-being of a place. And it is a reason why "We the People," not we the corporation or we the government, are the final arbiters—or should be. Because only people are capable of love; only people can incorporate multiple meanings of a place based on deep knowledge and an understanding that every place, and every being within a place, are in a constant state of evolution.

Wendell Berry writes eloquently about the relationship of rural people with place, and poet Gary Snyder writes about the human relationship with the wilderness. This mural reminded me that in the most troubled cities, too, people love their block, their school, a local gathering spot, or a neighborhood park. This is where life unfolds. Children hold in a deep part of their memory the smell, feel, and physicality of the places they grew up.

In this period of mass culture and hours of screen time, we are much more of and by our places than we acknowledge. When allowed to make choices, people can, and often do, take care of their place.

When Baraka was elected, a friend told me, people all over the city were exuberant, walking around greeting each other, "Hello, Mayor!" "Hello, Mayor!" Baraka had said, during his campaign, that when he was elected, everyone would be mayor.

Two years into his term, the mayor is pushing hard for policies that will bring greater shared prosperity to Newark. The murals are a sign of the rising spirits and the city's commitment to rebuilding the two model neighborhoods as a first step toward a genuine, inclusive renaissance.

Ithaca's Stories of Race

ITHACA, NEW YORK—As I drove across the Finger Lakes region of upstate New York, my little truck labored to climb the steep hills. Every so often I pulled over to allow the cars behind me to pass.

I was getting anxious about running out of time. It was the end of November, the weather was getting colder, and I had promised to be home by Christmas. If I headed straight back, I'd have nearly 2,700 miles to drive. But I wanted to swing south, through Louisiana, Texas, and the Southwest, so the trip would be much longer.

The decline of this area of New York State is striking. Homes are well worn, some have been restored, but many others are propped up with a few concrete blocks or tarped over. Many were surrounded by rusting RVs and cars.

And then there are the old barns. Many still provide shelter for animals and their feed, although daylight shone through the boards, and the structures seemed to be sinking in slow motion into the earth. The back of one barn was splayed out so that each stud was at a different angle, forming a fan. Another was propped up by poles stuck into the decaying walls, seeming to rest its weary bones on a walking stick.

Most of these towns appear to be predominantly white, as is Ithaca, which is 74 percent white.[1] In this progressive college town where a majority votes Democratic, few would identify the city as having issues of racial discord. White people, especially in the North, often reassure themselves that they are not racist and that issues of social justice are for others to worry about.

Racial segregation in the United States may actually be increasing, though. One indication is school attendance; the percentage of black students attending schools that are 90 percent minority or more increased from 34 percent in 1993 to 40 percent in 2013, according to a report by the Hillman Foundation.[2]

Ithaca's mirror

I met Godfrey L. Simmons Jr. and Sarah Chalmers in the second-story offices of the Workers Center, above the city's main street. We sat down at a table in their corner of this open space where nonprofits of all sorts use mismatched desks, tables, posters, books, and flyers in their quest for social change.

Simmons and Chalmers are a married couple as well as collaborators and founders of the Civic Ensemble; he's African American, and she's white. They have the gregarious personalities of theater people, combined with a habit of finishing each other's sentences.

The Civic Ensemble uses story circles to draw out the experiences and beliefs of the community; the narratives that emerge become the grist for their productions. A prompt from the organizers gets the sessions started. They might ask, When

Sarah Chalmers and Godfrey L. Simmons Jr. (left and right) are the founders of the Civic Ensemble; Jason Wilson (center) is a member of the cast for the production On the Corner.

have you felt unsafe? Or, Tell us about an encounter you had with the police.

Participants in the circle take turns telling their stories. Others listen. Having the chance to talk without interruption allows the stories to go deep and brings out the voices that are normally silent, and it makes it possible for them to address taboo topics.

"The people we work with tell the story of what it's like to be poor, what it's like to be a person of color walking down the street," Chalmers said.

A mom at one of these circles shared the experience of her two sons, African American middle schoolers, who missed their school bus. Not wanting to admit to their mom what happened, they decided to walk. But their school was far from home, and the route took them through a wealthy, white neighborhood where a woman who saw them called the police.

In this case, the story ended well—the officer quickly grasped the situation, called the boys' mother, and asked permission to take them to school. The mom was grateful, and all was well.

Still, there's the question of why a white woman would call the police on these two young boys. The Civic Ensemble explores that question in *On the Corner*, which was inspired by another, more dangerous incident that took place in Ithaca around the same time that Michael Brown was shot and killed in Ferguson, Missouri. A police officer, out of uniform, driving an unmarked car, ordered two black teenagers to the ground, with his gun drawn.

The community was outraged by the event and frightened by the possibility that the youths could have been killed. At a meeting, an African American elder said something that especially caught Chalmers's attention. As she remembers it, he stated, "The kids and the cops on the corner don't know where they came from. They don't understand the context of the script they're playing out."

Chalmers and Simmons decided that script was worth exploring.

In their fictionalized version, an African American teenager from the Bronx, "Julian," is sent to Ithaca by his mom to live with his aunt and uncle in order to keep him out of trouble. Several months later, his mother dies, and the distraught youth takes off walking. Not knowing where he's going, he wanders into the neighborhood described in the story circle, and an older white woman, "Mrs. Whitney," sees him and calls the police.

The play focuses on the interaction of Julian and the white

police officer who responds to the call. The officer quickly discovers that Julian's description matches that of a missing young person and urges him to return home. But Julian refuses, saying he won't go back until he understands how they got there—why was he stopped on the street when he was just walking? Why did someone call the police?

In the play, the white cop and the black teenager travel back in time to relive history, from the Wall Street slave markets of 1690 to a high school in the Bronx in 1978, bringing in racially charged events and references unique to Ithaca. The white woman who called the police is questioned, and she denies her action was racially motivated. In her defense, she tells the audience that she has even read Michelle Alexander's book on mass imprisonment, *The New Jim Crow*.

"The play welcomes everyone who recognizes themselves—whether you recognize the police officer or the young man or Mrs. Whitney—on the journey," Chalmers noted.

"It's not a play where a black teenager gets to learn and the cop is the savior," commented Simmons. "Nor is it a play where the black kid is the magic negro. There are two people who represent a binary of people who are ignorant of how we got here."

Ithaca residents contributed to the play from start to finish: They shared their stories and transcribed the recordings, and many participated in follow-up sessions that helped to flesh out the details of the play. Community members made up the acting ensemble and the audience, and some stayed afterward for discussion.

Jason Wilson, a member of the *On the Corner* cast, joined us at the Workers Center as we talked. Wilson has short cropped hair and wore a black leather bomber jacket. Performing as part of the cast "helped me break down a few walls within myself," he said. "You don't build that kind of comradery in a machine

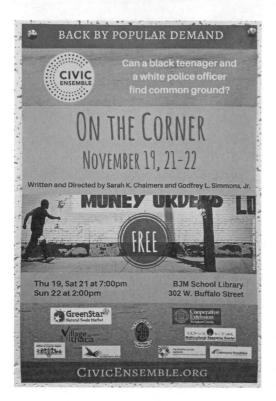

Ithaca residents helped create the Civic Ensemble's production of On the Corner.

shop—you're putting yourself out there with other people, you have each other's back, you try to be there for each other on stage and off. I feel more a part of a community here, rather than how one might feel, invisible or whatever."

The experience in the theater shifts the conversation on taboo topics like race and class, explained Simmons. "People can have conversations that they might not have anywhere else."

We know that the way society is structured is not okay, Chalmers said. "It's not okay that some people can't eat, and that some people don't get to learn, and some don't have a shelter."

To build a different sort of world, Chalmers said, we have to hear one another—to understand the experiences of people in our community, including those we rarely spend time with. And we need to allow ourselves the space to imagine something else, to remember that we do have the power. Society "is something we made. But we can make something else," she said. "When we create a play, we practice making something else."

"What we make, and how we make it, matters," she said. "And it changes us."

• • •

In each of the places I visited during this part of my trip, people were intentionally taking on racism and white supremacy, but in a way unique to that community's circumstances and capacities. In Greensboro, truth and reconciliation, a civil rights

Historical marker in Greensboro, North Carolina.

museum, a plaque commemorating a massacre, story circles, and a black-owned food cooperative are all means of creating a different story of what it means to be black or white in that city. In Harrisonburg, the police are learning from the EMU community of peacebuilders how to use restorative justice to build relationships of respect and understanding. In Newark, a mayor who came from the black community is working to rebuild the city, not so it can bring in new, wealthier, and whiter residents, but so the people already there can thrive. And in Appalachia, a radio program that connects prison inmates to those they love helps humanize the incarcerated residents of the hill country. And resistance to yet another new prison is calling into question an economic development strategy based on holding thousands of people, especially people of color, behind bars.

In community, we can comprehend each other more fully as complex, multifaceted human beings, and perhaps we become harder to stereotype. We can share stories, and over time those stories can build into a common understanding of who we are in all of our diversity. Then, perhaps, a new inclusive story can emerge—one that can take us into a more just future. Maybe, even, to a beloved community.

IV. Home, via Texas
and the Southwest

Dallas at Christmas and a Syrian Family

I pulled into Dallas, Texas, on December 5. I had picked out a room on Airbnb and landed at an older, welcoming, two-story home. My friendly and proud Texas host directed me to a good local coffee shop and a part of the city where I might find a walkable shopping district.

As it happened, my arrival coincided with the planned arrival of a Syrian refugee family. But they were stranded in New York. The arrival of two small children, their parents, and two grandparents had evoked much consternation.

A few weeks earlier, Governor Greg Abbott had announced that Texas would not accept any refugees from Syria, and on December 2 his administration had filed an injunction to prevent the family of six from settling in Dallas. He then relented and withdrew his motion but still demanded that the federal government provide more information about the Syrians.

Syrian immigrants are not the only ones provoking fear. Outside a mosque in Irving, Texas, a camouflage-clad group armed with rifles showed up during services on November 21, chanting against the "Islamization" of America. Irving, a suburb of Dallas, became famous when Ahmed Mohamed, a 14-year-old student, was arrested for bringing a homemade clock to school. The Texas Rebel Knights, a Ku Klux Klan group from Quinlan, Texas, announced they would hold a rally outside the Irving mosque on December 12.

The Christian leaders in Dallas were divided on how to respond to Muslims in general, to Muslim refugees, and to anti-Muslim protests.

"I believe it is time for us to lay aside political correctness," Reverend Robert Jeffress, pastor of the First Baptist Church of Dallas, had told his congregation a few weeks earlier. I watched the service online from my Airbnb. "Islam is a false religion, and it is inspired by Satan himself," he said. The parishioners sitting in the pews of the crowded church applauded loudly.

There is another side to the city's Christian community, though. On December 6, the Sunday after I arrived, I attended two services of congregations known for open-mindedness. What I found was a commitment among these Christians to live out the hospitable, compassionate side of Christianity and to do all they could to welcome strangers.

The 9 a.m. service at the Cathedral of Hope, one of the largest LGBTQ churches in the country, was filled with couples, mainly men, who came to the church for worship and—if the minister's language was any indication—for acceptance. All are welcome to take communion here, he told the congregation. As I watched men file to the front of the giant church, I could only imagine how rare that acceptance had been in their lives.

The Cathedral of Hope's welcome extends to Latinos as well; in addition to two services in English, there is one service held in Spanish every Sunday.

After the services, the parishioners gathered in the Fellowship Hall for coffee and pastries. I asked Reverend Todd Scoggins for his view of the Syrian refugees. "Oh, we would welcome them!" he said without hesitation. "We know what it's like to experience discrimination."

Reverend Neil G. Cazares-Thomas, senior pastor of the 4,500-member church, also made clear that the refugee family would be welcome in his church and in Dallas. "Even if we had to defy the governor, we would welcome them," he told me. Cazares-Thomas, born into a Mormon family in England, is married to his partner, Isaiah Thomas-Cazares, and the two are raising a child.

Cazares-Thomas said that he and other members of his church were mobilizing to stand outside the Irving mosque on

Reverend Wes Magruder holds a small bowl filled with coins collected by a child in his congregation as a gift for a Syrian refugee family.

the following Saturday to support the Muslims who were being targeted by the KKK.

I drove my truck-camper across town, arriving just as the service of the First Methodist Church of Kessler Park was set to begin. Reverend Wes Magruder wasted little time in speaking to the refugee issue and the duty of Christians to welcome them. In one emotional moment during the service, he brought out a small, yellow plastic bowl partly filled with coins. He said that a first-grader, named Emma Rodriguez, a member of the congregation, had handed him her collection of coins worth $3.64 to help the Syrian refugee family. He invited his congregation to join him outside the Irving mosque on Saturday to counter the anti-Muslim protesters.

Shortly after, the Syrian family quietly slipped into the city, without news cameras or reporters.

I wanted to stay to see what would happen at the planned protest and counter-protest at the mosque in Irving the following weekend, but time was short before I was expected at home in Suquamish, Washington, and I needed to keep moving west. I later read in the *Dallas Morning News*[1] that the Klan had called off the protest rally, or, rather, delayed it until the following year. Mosque leaders in Irving then requested that the counter-demonstration take place elsewhere and invited local religious leaders to meet with them quietly, out of the national press spotlight. The demonstration, which became the United Against Racism and Hate march, took place at Fair Park in Dallas, with hundreds in attendance.

Childbirth and Transcendence

West across Texas, the flat, open country continued, hour after hour. Then, just outside Amarillo, as dusk was settling, the land suddenly dropped into a canyon formed by the Prairie Dog Town Fork of the Red River. In that canyon, near the river, I camped for the night, watching the sunset light up the sky. Later, the brightest stars I'd seen during the trip came out. And in the morning, I hiked along a sandy path next to the river, along crumbly cliff faces, crossing dry washes, encountering a flock of quail browsing unafraid in the underbrush.

Hours later, as I approached Santa Fe, New Mexico, I saw a man walking along the highway, carrying a big duffle bag.

So many people are on the move, disconnected from place, with no one who can support them. Sometimes we call them homeless, or refugees, or the displaced, as though a label protects us from being one of them. Any of us could become homeless, especially in a country where an illness can result in bankruptcy, or a home can be lost due to a layoff or speculation in mortgage-backed securities. Over time, if climate change

makes portions of our coastlines and the Southwest uninhabit-
able, millions of us may find ourselves on the move.

Many religious traditions tell us to treat strangers with kind-
ness and to feed, clothe, and shelter them. There's a moral right-
ness about that advice, but there's also the reality that none of us
is secure unless other people will care for us in times of need.

After these months on the road, I was acutely aware of how
much it meant to me to know I would find a friendly face at my
next stop.

SAN ILDEFONSO PUEBLO, NEW MEXICO—Migration in
some form has probably always been part of human existence,
but it hasn't always been a lonely venture.

In the Southwest, I visited several pueblos of the Tewa people, whose ancestors migrated south hundreds of miles from
Mesa Verde, in what is now Colorado, to northern New Mexico,
probably because of changes in climate patterns.

Thomas Gonzales, a member of the San Ildefonso Pueblo,
north of Santa Fe, told me stories about how his Tewa ancestors
migrated to places where rivers converged, where water sup-
plies would be more reliable. He said that villages would send
out small groups to set up the next village, and over the course
of generations, the Tewa people would move across the high
desert.

Thomas and Nicolle Gonzales invited me to visit their
home in San Ildefonso Pueblo, where many of the Tewa people
still live in one- and two-story adobe homes that surround a
central plaza. The interior shade keeps the homes cool during
the hot, sunny days. At night, the warmed walls radiate the heat,
maintaining a comfortable temperature inside.

Outside of town, on two sides, are small hills. Those used
to be the goals when people played ball in the plaza, Tom told

Thomas and Nicolle Gonzales.

me. It could take all day for a team to get the ball up to the top of one hill while the other team battled to get it back and take it up the opposite slope.

These desert people learned, over many years, how and when to plant crops; what to plant on top of the high mesas and what to plant in the valleys; how to make the best use of the moisture; and how to best combine crops.

And they knew when and where to hunt. "Right after it snowed a few days back, my dad said, 'Let's go,'" Gonzales explained. Tracks in the fresh snow would reveal where the deer or elk had passed.

Birthing center as healing

I had come to this part of New Mexico to meet Nicolle Gonzales, a Navajo nurse-midwife who is bringing back traditional Native American birthing practices. Gonzales is planning a birthing center where mothers can feel the full support of their families and communities and reconnect to the traditions that offer them strength, healing, and sureness.

Gonzales suggested that I visit during one of her days off from the Los Alamos clinic where she currently practices as a midwife. We met at the home she shares with her husband and three children, on a quiet back street.

Gonzales has the strength of a runner, which she is, and the confidence and authority that comes with calming nervous moms-to-be and guiding them through difficult labors. As her children played in the next room, Nicolle and I talked at the kitchen table, with Tom occasionally adding comments.

The confidence I saw in Nicolle was hard won. She gave birth to her first child, Charlotte, at age 20, and the experience left her feeling disconnected and lost. She recalled her labor in a noisy, crowded hospital room with relatives talking to each other and on their phones, a doctor who wouldn't answer her questions, and, in the end, so much blood loss that she nearly lost consciousness.

"That birth was very traumatic and loud," she said.

The feeling of being out of control carried over into her early mothering. "I just didn't feel connected to being a mom for the first couple years. When we look at some photos of me as a young mom, Tom always says I look so checked out. I didn't know how to be a mother. I was very impressionable and wanted to please everybody, like these young girls do," she said.

"So I want to support women when they're in that vulnerable state."

Nicolle was raised within Navajo traditions. Her mother had attended one of the residential schools where many Native children were taken from their families and traditions, sometimes by force or coercion, and many were abused. Her mother married into a large family, and her mother-in-law taught her to cook and sew. She loved it. Still, Nicolle's grandparents were alcoholics, and they got divorced because her grandfather was abusive. "Nobody really taught my mom how to be a mom," Nicolle said.

Nicolle wants her birthing center to help women heal from the trauma that is so common in Indian country. And, by reconnecting them to their culture and community, she wants to help prepare them psychologically and spiritually to be good mothers.

"I want women to have that connection and be happy and proud of their accomplishment," she explained. "I want to create a space where they feel confident and can give birth in a way that feels good to them, so they can experience their power." This is especially important for women who have experienced sexual abuse, which, Nicolle told me, had also been part of her past.

"I had one woman who was so traumatized, she came into the office shaking," Nicolle said "She was pregnant purposefully, but when she came in, there was sweat on her lip, and she was like, 'What are you going to do to me?'" The birth process can retrigger abuse trauma, Nicolle noted, because the women feel, once again, out of control.

Nicolle's approach is to give these survivors as much control as possible over the birth process. "I sat down lower than her and we talked, and I explained what would happen, and I asked permission all the time: 'What do you want to do? Can I touch you?' ... It feels like a victory for them, and for me, when they've had their baby and it's not traumatizing to them, and they feel in control. You see the shift through the whole pregnancy as that confidence sets in and it's like, hey, I can do this. I've done it!"

Buffalo Dance

Nicolle, Tom, and their children took me with them to see the annual Buffalo Dance at the plaza of the nearby Tesuque Pueblo. In the icy cold of a short December day, the men and women drummed and danced to the four directions in a celebration that lasted for hours.

Later, we returned to the Gonzaleses' home for fry bread and Indian tacos, and to talk more about the birthing center.

"When you think about birth, it's like a ceremony," Nicolle said. "There's sacrifice, there's pain, and there's healing."

During the long pueblo dances, women learn to draw on their inner strengths, Nicolle said, and that can help them get through a difficult childbirth.

"The Corn Dance is in August. You dance nonstop, usually without shoes on, and it's hot and you're exhausted," she said. "You're listening to that drum to lead you through.

"I use that example. I tell them, this is like the Corn Dance. You're tired, but you're listening to that drum. You're almost done. The baby's gonna be here."

Nicolle wants her birth center to incorporate that sense of ceremony. She imagines a place that feels like home and is dimly lit, with cedar burning. There is drumming if the mom wants it, with people in the community there to welcome the baby. She envisions a place where pregnant women can bring photos of their grandmothers, where traditional herbs and teas are part of the healing. She wants the young moms to be able to choose to have the first words spoken to their baby be in their native language.

To be the sort of caregiver the women can count on, Nicolle does her own spiritual work. For her, participating in the dances is "kind of a rebirth, a recentering.

"In our Navajo culture, teaching our mind is very powerful, so we talk about *hozho*, which is walking in beauty, or being positive, and we understand that what we say can manifest into reality."

She urges the women to prepare spiritually for birth and motherhood by praying and participating in ceremonies. "We remind them that it is important to take care of themselves and their baby and family. That you are connected to something larger than what is just happening to you right now."

Research on adverse childhood experiences shows how critical the first months of life are.[1] Abuse, neglect, or violence in the home can increase the likelihood of poor emotional and cognitive development, risky behavior in adolescence, diseases in adulthood, and an early death. Native people are survivors of multiple generations of trauma, making these early interactions between mother and child all the more critical. When a mother has strong relationships with other adults, she is best able to provide the safe and loving upbringing the child requires to thrive, according to the Center for Disease Control and Prevention. For women in abusive relationships, or women who are smoking or using drugs or alcohol, pregnancy is a time they are especially open to turning their lives around, Nicolle said. Connecting to their traditions and to family and community can make the difference. The sort of support the mother receives isn't the only factor that determines whether the child will feel fully connected, fully loved, but it is an important one. "It's not just work, as my mom said. It's enjoying being a mom, which I'm just now getting a handle on," Nicolle said. "I want women to have that connection and be happy and proud of their accomplishments." I left the pueblo that night with the sound of the drumming still in my ears, imagining what it will mean for young mothers to give birth with all this support, and for the children born to these mothers. This birth center could serve as a powerful source of healing from intergenerational trauma.

Driving north

The weather was turning cold, and the first snow of my travels arrived. I camped at Los Ojos Hot Springs, soaking in the pools and hiking in the nearby hills. An old village site still contained shards of ancient pottery, hinting at the artistry of previous inhabitants.

I thought about healing and the sorts of connection we need to be fully whole, including the connection to our own sense of self. We can get distracted by what advertisers tell us we should want, or by peer pressure. But when we achieve clarity about what's important, we become more focused.

I thought back to what my friend and host in Detroit, Ma Teresa Lomeli Penman, told me when I asked her where she thinks power comes from. Penman is an immigrant from Mexico and a community organizer in Detroit's Latino community. She said, "It's when your head, and your heart, and your hands are aligned. Then you know what you are doing, and your clarity makes you powerful."

It was time to head north, but I was worried about snow. I

Shards of ancient pottery near Los Ojos Hot Springs, New Mexico.

pored over weather maps and road conditions reports and then drove on.

Snow outlined each layer of geological rocks and the up-swell of hills. The contours of the adobe houses, junk trucks, and birdbaths in the yards were also delineated by snow. I could see dark clouds touching down on the hilltops to the east; the weather service was reporting blizzard-like conditions there. I felt fortunate to be skirting just to the west of the storm.

The road north was through dry, open country. I drove past the turnoff of Mesa Verde, stopped at another ancient village site off the main road, and then marveled as the craggy land-scape turned to red rock, with the high cliffs and stunning rock formations of the Utah desert.

Moab—A Bridge

When I arrived in Moab, Utah, in mid-December, people were talking not about the upcoming Christmas holidays, but about the Day of the Dead festival that had happened six weeks earlier. The event is an annual fund-raiser for the Moab Valley Multicultural Center, a nonprofit formed to serve minority populations in Moab, especially the region's Latino immigrants.

The Day of the Dead is a traditional Mexican holiday, celebrated on November 1 and 2, when families gather to remember loved ones. But the occasion is far from somber. In the yard of the multicultural center, volunteers and staff created a celebratory graveyard, with altars on the graves, and even a small pet cemetery. A band played, a brightly festooned skull hung above the crowd, and there was traditional food and a children's dance performance.

"It was amazing," Rhiana Medina, executive director of the center, told me. "The people we have helped through all sorts of difficult situations helped us put on this event, and it always takes me aback how much they are willing to do."

The event was launched as a fund-raiser, but it does much more than raise money. People from south of the border celebrate and share their culture and keep their traditions alive. And, amid the grinning skeletons and bright colors, the festival serves as a reminder of something profound and universal— the preciousness and finiteness of life.

"We do everything we can to keep [the celebration] connected to the indigenous roots—the circle of life; how life comes up out of the ground, and then as it dies it goes back into the ground," Medina explained. "We bless the earth before we build altars on the tombs, and all of the components of a traditional indigenous altar are very carefully placed on every tomb."

Rhiana Medina at the Moab Valley Multicultural Center.

This celebration, with its embrace of life and the inevitability of death, is one of the gifts the multicultural center offers the larger community.

Death is taboo in American culture. Many of us have never seen someone die, except in the sanitized versions shown in the movies. Perhaps that's why we fear death.

I had seen the smiling skeletons in shops and in the art of Mexico and Central America, and at first I found the imagery unpleasant and macabre. But over time, I came to appreciate the little figurines riding a motorcycle or dancing in front of an orchestra of skeletons. Life is ephemeral, they seem to say. Enjoy it while you still have flesh on those bones!

Rhiana Medina has a lot of experience connecting across cultures. She grew up in northern Minnesota. Her father is part Native and part Mexican; her mother is Scandinavian. She inherited dark hair, olive skin, and an easy laugh. "My sisters, because we're all mixed, look different," she said. "A lot of people would ask, 'Is that your mom?'"

To further confuse things, her dad didn't want his children to speak Spanish. "He thought it would make us sound uneducated.

"I have a foot in two cultures," she said. The mission of the center is likewise to build bridges between cultures. This is a tough challenge in a place like Moab. Many Anglo residents are leery of the Spanish-speaking immigrants. And many, although not all, are wealthy. Moab is within a few miles of Arches and Canyonlands National Parks and on the Colorado River. A large number of the white people who come to the area are there to enjoy the spectacular scenery and outdoor activities. Most of the immigrants came for jobs at hotels and restaurants.

"If you're a refugee because of violence, or economic reasons, or climate change, you didn't want to move. It wasn't like you wanted to uproot and leave your family, and your home, and your lifestyle, and your culture and move thousands of miles away," Medina said. "You did it because you were forced to.

"It does cause stresses on the places that receive the migrants," she acknowledged. "It's stressful in the schools and on the economy. But not blaming the people is a good place to start."

So how do you build bridges between people whose life experiences are so different?

"To have other people trust you, you have to let people know you," Medina said. "We're out in the community, we are good neighbors, we volunteer at other people's organizations. If you want friends, you have to be a friend."

The center's other big event is "Dancing with the Moab Stars," a performance and fund-raiser featuring prominent community leaders.

"We start by asking local leaders and celebrities to risk making fools of themselves by getting up onstage and dancing in front of the whole community," she laughed. "This is asking a lot!"

Mural at the Moab Valley Multicultural Center.

The first year, the mayor and the sheriff danced. The next year, the CEO of the hospital and local business owners got up onstage.

"This was during the height of the tourist season, and they are probably working 12 hours a day. And we're saying, 'Hey, want to be in a dance show when you have three months to learn a routine with this person you don't know, and you probably have no dance experience, and you'll perform it as a public dance competition for a good cause?'"

The Moab stars are not all local celebrities. They could include a Hispanic couple who have been in Moab for a long time but are not known outside their immediate circle. "The audience reads their bio in the program and learns who these wonderful people are.

"I have seen, in six years, a transformation of this place from being leery of the multicultural center helping 'those' people," Medina said, "to getting more community support."

In 2015, the center took a leap of faith and moved the fundraiser into the largest indoor venue in town, the 700-seat high school auditorium. And they filled it. That turnout is pretty good for an event where the monologue goes back and forth between English and Spanish, and there are no big outside celebrities—just the people of the community in costume, doing dance routines they recently learned, willing to compete, laugh, and possibly look foolish.

• • •

More people are displaced than have been at any time in human history—some 60 million are fleeing violent conflict alone, according to the United Nations.[1] Additional millions are on the move for economic reasons or, increasingly, because of climate change.

At a time when so many people are forced to relocate, it may seem odd to celebrate place-based community. But reconnecting to a place, and to the other people who comprise it, gives us power whether we (or they) have just arrived or have lived there a lifetime.

I think about the immigrants I met in Detroit, Cincinnati, Prospect, Kentucky, and Moab, and the vitality, work ethic, pageantry, and warmth they brought with them. And I think about how many more of us will likely be displaced in the future, whether because a rising sea inundates our freshwater supply or because of drought, heat, or flooding—or because we lose a job or a home. We don't know if we will be the ones displaced, or if our community will be taking in those who are displaced. But with the amount of carbon already in the atmosphere, we can be pretty sure that people will continue to be moving.

How well will we as a society cope with that much disruption? The kind of world we inhabit in the coming years—whether it's one of resilience or a dystopian game of survival—may depend more than anything on how well we welcome the stranger.

Relationship to Self

A Culture of Connection	An Economy of Extraction
Align head, hands, and heart.	Yearn for more stuff.
Fulfill your potential.	Fit into the economy as a worker, consumer, and taxpayer.
Take responsibility for family, the larger community, and future generations.	Be responsible to myself and my family.
Health and development are primary.	Financial wealth is primary.
Each life (human and otherwise) is sacred.	Nothing is sacred.

The Power of Connection

WARM SPRINGS, OREGON—It's dark. It has been dark for hours. I'm winding up a long road off the main highway on my way to a campsite in the Cascade Mountains east of Portland, Oregon, just one day before I'm due to get back home. My eyes are foggy after driving all day into snow and rain, and then for hours into headlights in the December dark.

Now, though, I'd be happy to see someone. I haven't passed another car since I turned off the main highway, and the road is getting icier by the mile. I round a curve and see the lights of a town far below. The ice on the road catches in my headlights and glitters up at me menacingly.

Then I notice something. A half-moon offers just a glimpse beyond the headlights. I am following a creek, and snowy mountain slopes appear on both sides of the road. And there are trees, a sure sign I'm nearly home. In fact, these are the most trees I've seen since I left Louisiana!

The moon goes in and out, behind the clouds, lighting the hills and then fading. When I finally pull into a spot in a deserted campsite on this nearly Christmas night, the stars are out, and the tree-covered, snow-covered mountainsides are clear, lit by moonlight.

I step out of my truck, into the crisp night air.

Albert Einstein said, "There are two ways to live: you can live as if nothing is a miracle; you can live as if everything is a miracle."

I think about my white-knuckle drive up the mountain, and the frost, and the fear, and the self-recrimination for choosing a dangerous route. And I realize that I can choose to remember this moment for its crystalline beauty or for its danger, for its cold or for its clarity.

For the moment, I am grateful for the blessing of a warm camper to retreat to and this chance to stand, fully alive, in the cold, still starlight.

Untethered

The last day on the road, I woke up in the dark at my campsite high in the Cascade Mountains, eager to finish this final leg of what has turned out to be a 12,000-mile journey. I shivered as I dressed, scraped the ice off the windshield, and, without stopping to boil water for coffee, headed off through the dark.

When I finally hit the main highway, the pavement seemed dry and clear. But then snow started—first rain, then snow so thick I had to turn the headlight beams low in order to see. The road surface turned from snow to ice, the road frighteningly slick. It was a relief, after some time, to finally reach the climbers' hut at the pass where I found coffee and a break from the weather.

This was my fourth day traveling through storms, through

lonely landscapes where I knew no one. I thought about what it means to be untethered from family, place, and other people.

Sometimes it can be liberating—to meet the expectations of family and community, we can get stuck in old, unhappy patterns that restrict us, preventing our full flowering. A hug is both love and constraint; we are nourished and held back.

For me, being away meant letting go of schedules and multitasking. I gladly listened to people's stories as they slowly unfolded, watching the speakers with fresh eyes, noting their excitement. I wanted to hear what was real for them without an overlay of my assumptions about the world. I allowed myself spontaneity; I stayed an extra day or two or three if I wanted to learn more. So I enjoyed the freedom of being on the road, knowing that, in the end, home and loved ones were waiting.

In ancient times, though, banishment could mean death. Solitary confinement can bring on insanity.

And isolation is everywhere in our extraction-based culture. We are expected to leave our family and community to chase a job opportunity. Being attached to a place is seen as backwards and romantic. We should be ready to move to make way for a mine or a highway, to sacrifice a mountain or a creek or a neighborhood park to extract coal or to expedite truck traffic.

Inequality increases the isolation. With this country's steep and growing divide between rich and poor, many believe they can't afford to spend time building a deep connection to community, extended family, or their own soul's yearning if that might interfere with earning a living. They believe it's their fault if they haven't achieved the lifestyles they see portrayed on television. The penalty for those who fail to climb the ever-steeper ladder is not only poverty; it is also shame. And shame undercuts our capacity to offer or ask for the support we need to get back on our feet.

This sort of isolation is debilitating.

We evolved to live in communities that offer mutual support. Each of us, born naked and vulnerable, relies on our mother and the people who support her. It really does take a village. We crave connection from the first time our infant eyes seek out the eyes of another. It continues throughout life, this craving for connection. Small children separated from loving caregivers wither and may die, even if their physical needs are met. The adolescent transition to adulthood is all about understanding oneself in relationship to peers. Adults may believe they can tough it out on their own, but we all need the connections of family and friends to thrive.

Other species, too, evolved in relationships that are miraculous and worthy of respect, even when we don't fully understand them. I think back to Steve Charter's excitement about the soil-based ecosystems that could thrive on his ranch, conserving rainfall and absorbing carbon from the atmosphere. Large and small, the beings we share this world with are capable of extraordinary things, like turning sunlight into food, blanketing our planet with temperature-stabilizing gases, exhaling the oxygen we need to breathe, cleaning the water and the soil, turning dead matter into new life, even keeping our guts healthy—these nonhuman species make life possible, and our continued existence depends on them.

We can flourish without riches, but not without connection. Yet the extraction mindset teaches that we must sacrifice the very things that bring joy—time with people we love, a sense of belonging, creativity for its own sake, the natural world—for the values of extraction: money and power.

Give me a place to stand

As I drove through the cold early morning, my last day on the road, I thought about what I'd learned as I traveled those 12,000 miles. For too long we have allowed giant corporations to move through our communities like giant bulldozers, pushing people and nature around, and leaving behind chaos and debris.

In our communities, though, we can create real transformation.

I thought about the people I met in forgotten Rust Belt cities and in rural Appalachia, in Newark, and on the Turtle Mountain Reservation—people who see that it is up to them.

I met a doctor, ranchers, artists, factory workers and farmers, a midwife, and a police officer who are creating new possibilities for their communities. I found places I'd mistakenly written off as wastelands that are, in fact, deeply loved by those who live there, and I learned that those people are committed to recovering their places' beauty and vitality.

By coming together, we can take care of each other, ourselves, and the natural world. Deepening our knowledge and collaboration, we can expand our power so that it is "we the people"—not the corporations—who determine what happens in our neighborhoods and ecosystems. We can cultivate gardens, the arts, celebration, and good food; we can protect the wild and the many creatures that live there, as well as our neighborhoods. We can create our own livelihoods and exchanges.

Archimedes said, give me a place to stand, and I can move the earth. When we have a solid community, we have that place to stand. We have the authority of the ranchers and Native people of southeast Montana and the tribes along the West Coast who are working together to stop new fossil fuel infrastructure. We have the political clout to elect someone who puts the common good first, as the people of Newark, New Jersey, did when they elected Ras Baraka as mayor. We know ourselves and our culture, and what matters to us, as the people in Detroit are discovering. We have our own stories, as the theater group in Ithaca knows, and the people in Greensboro have struggled so hard to establish. And we have what we need to build our own economic foundation, to meet our own needs. We know the ecosystems we are part of, the flow of the water and the seasons, and we have the most at stake to defend them.

To a people deeply connected to a homeland, there are no throw-away people, and there are no sacrifice zones. All people and all places are sacred.

When a young person gets into trouble, instead of throwing him or her into an uncaring juvenile lock-up, the community can gather around, offering restorative justice, deep listening, high expectations, and adult guidance.

When people need livelihoods, we can join together to create and support locally rooted enterprises, cooperatives, and financial institutions, so that our resources can go back into the local economy and form a virtuous cycle of investment and re-investment.

We can use natural resources in ways that do not ask more of delicate ecosystems than they can withstand. Harvesting, gathering, and extracting with respect and care mean that our children and their children will be able to do the same.

Our society is becoming increasingly unstable; collapse is possible, as is the possibility of localized breakdowns, especially with a divisive and violent political climate and so many extreme weather events.

Here, too, community is the answer. When things are really hard, we have a far better chance of escaping trauma if we turn to each other, rather than turn *on* each other. Communities that have practiced getting things done have strengthened that collaborative muscle, which makes other work possible. Communities that have a practice of reaching across dividing lines have a better chance of avoiding the paranoia and violence of racism. Instead, whether in times of duress or in ordinary life, they can draw on all diverse talents and form a whole much stronger than the sum of the parts.

Why place-based revolution?

Revolutionaries of the past have looked for something grand, something more important than community-level change. And there are good reasons, today, for wanting change to come quickly and to come big.

But change that starts from the bottom up is more like evolution, drawing on the full complexity of who we are. That complexity is possible in the rich networks of interaction with people that happens at the local level. Face to face, we are less likely to stereotype each other or resort to oversimplified ideologies.

This sort of place-based power is showing up in communities like Cincinnati that are building cooperatives in collaboration with the trade union movement and the faith community. In southeast Montana, where ranchers and Native people who love that place joined forces to defeat a massive coal strip mine. In Detroit, where neighborhood activism is challenging policies of abandonment and making room for a new society to flower. On the Turtle Mountain Reservation, where tribal members chose pure water forever over a short-term fracking windfall, and where the tribe is now developing clean energy resources. Place-based power is being born in Whitesburg, Kentucky, where a people written off as ignorant victims of a collapsing coal industry are reclaiming their culture, their landscape, and their economy. It is happening in Moab, Utah, where appreciation for differences in culture and life experience is opening doors and changing minds.

The hitch, of course, is that all these communities reclaiming their futures, their land and resources, will interfere with the ability of giant corporations to take resources, game our financial system, and outsource jobs. So they will do their best to stop us. They'll bring out their economists, who will claim that our ideas will fail. They'll pay off politicians and sponsor PACs and think tanks to get their guys in office. They'll cast doubt on the science of climate change, and stymie policies that phase out fossil fuel extraction. And they will dismiss our efforts as small and insignificant.

They will do this not because evil people are in charge, but because our system offers huge rewards for continuing the extraction, and big penalties for stepping out of that system.

Ultimately, we will need to change the laws that favor big, transnational extractive companies over enterprises that are locally rooted and locally contributing. The economy will need to come back to being a servant of people, not our master.

Our work, then, involves creating both inclusive, life-sustaining communities and the systems change that will allow them to thrive. To prevail, we will have to make common cause with communities doing this work around the country and around the world. This type of globalization is the opposite of that promoted by big corporations and written into international trade deals. It is people-to-people, community-to-community—no one gets power over others or gets to extract wealth from others. The relationships are among equals, each grounded in their own place.

In place-based communities, we can build trust so that we

can let go of the old world and embrace possibilities for a new world, even when that new world remains a mystery.

Sometimes the work of building community seems too hard. Without the skills and cultural norms, even the best-intentioned work can break down. Utopias do not exist. And yet, communities of place are where we can find our true selves, our power, and our best hopes.

If we do find ways to work together, we may discover that, out of the chaos and the not knowing, there is sustenance. There is a way forward. We can't find it by turning our power over to big, outside forces. And we can't do it alone. But by taking action together, beginning in place-based communities, we actually can change the world, one place at a time.

101 Ways to Reclaim Local Power

There are no one-size-fits-all ways to build communities. Instead, many, many approaches exist, any one of which can make a difference. The people living in a particular place know which ones are right for them—or they can figure it out if they talk and listen to each other.

This list incorporates some approaches we've published in *YES! Magazine* and ones I learned about on my road trip. Some are major projects that require months of building skills and hard work. Others are simple things you can do tomorrow without breaking a sweat. All of them can help make communities more just, ecologically sustainable, inclusive, and supportive.

Think of this as a brainstorm list to spark your own ideas and imagination.

Build Bridges

1   Learn about the original people whose land you live on. Acknowledge them.

2   Walk. Pause to talk with people you encounter.

3 Find out who in your community is not free—buried in debt, in prison, being trafficked. Support their vision of liberation, or, at least, help them connect.

4 Attend someone else's ceremony or celebration.

5 Find out the names and stories of the people on your block. Share yours.

6 Convene talking circles to bring together groups that don't normally interact: old and young, police and community, victims and offenders, people of different races.

7 Make space for everyone to speak for themselves, especially those often silenced or marginalized.

8 If you normally talk a lot, listen more than you talk. If you are usually quiet, take the risk of speaking.

9 Get to know the people who are just arriving in your community, especially refugees, and find out where they came from, why they left their place of birth, and their current circumstances.

10 Offer translation at community events.

11 Create a truth and reconciliation commission to get a shared understanding of local traumatizing events.

12 Get to know young people. Do they plan to remain in the area? What would make it possible for them to stay? What would they like to offer?

13 Connect school and criminal justice officials to restorative justice training and resources. Convene conversations about how and why to use restorative justice methods.

14 Celebrate youth who are working for the common good. Connect them to the elders so that both sides can learn and grow.

15 Find out who in your community is homeless; form a group to offer connection and support.

16 Join the Rotary, Kiwanis, Masons, or another service organization, and invite in others who represent the full spectrum of your community.

17 Organize a film series featuring the histories of various groups that make up your community, and follow up with discussions about local implications.

18 Form alliances across racial, cultural, language, and other differences via sister faith groups or sister neighborhoods.

19 Make films featuring the people, history, and cultures of your community. Collaborate with the subjects of the films on how they are framed and presented.

20 Introduce talking circles to schools so students learn a safe way to be heard and to resolve conflicts.

21 Find out who from your community is incarcerated. Help keep them connected with the community, and make a plan to safely reincorporate them in the community upon their release.

22 Hold celebrations featuring the diverse foods, music, dance, and art from the cultures and traditions that make up your community.

23 Ask for help. (Don't be a martyr!) People often want to pitch in but aren't sure how. Create spaces for leadership to emerge.

Connect to Your Ecological Home

24 Learn where your drinking water comes from, how it gets to homes, schools, and businesses, and how (and whether) the system is keeping water safe, clean, and well supplied.

25 Turn waste into a resource #1: Set up a worker-owned cooperative to deconstruct buildings, instead of demolishing them, and to reuse the materials.

26 Turn waste into a resource #2: Harvest unwanted fruits and vegetables, and distribute them to neighbors or food banks, or make them into juices and sauces.

27 Turn waste into a resource #3: Turn food scraps and yard waste into compost that can transform degraded dirt into living, carbon-absorbing, water-retaining, fertile soil.

28 Reclaim unused land for farming and foraging.

29 Start a food forest.

30 Organize a cleanup day to remove invasive plants and trash.

31 Open a wilderness school to share the skills of wild crafting, permaculture, wilderness navigation, and foraging.

32 Learn about the resident birds and wildlife, where they raise their young, and which ones migrate through.

33 Create conservation easements or land trusts to maintain green space, but allow compatible human uses, such as foraging, hiking, and farming.

34   Clean and conserve water by creating wetlands and rain gardens.

35   Learn about the links between soil health and human health.

36   Hold plant and seed exchanges to share heritage plant species.

37   Grow food, whether in a single pot on a balcony or on an urban farm.

Connect to Self:
Build Creative, Healing, and Sacred Spaces

38   Identify and acknowledge your elders, especially those with a concern for the greater good.

39   Gently acknowledge trauma, yours and others'.

40   Acknowledge that many forms of trauma cross generations and arrive in ways you may not understand—some a result of racism, sexism, or homophobia; some from war, sexual assault, or childhood abuse or neglect.

41   Recognize that traumatized people need to define for themselves what they require to heal, and they don't need to be second-guessed or "helped."

42   Align your heart, head, and hands, so you know what you're doing and why.

43   Know your own values and how you came to them— what you believe in, what matters most. Allow them to evolve, especially via encounters with others.

44   Share your favorite tradition and its meaning with people from other traditions.

45   Meet for coffee with someone who is feeling isolated.

46   Create sacred (or at least safe) times and spaces for contemplation and healing.

47   Convert a defunct warehouse or old theater into an arts cooperative with living/working spaces, plus teaching, rehearsal, and performance spaces.

48   Hold an annual harvest festival.

49   Celebrate the growers, processors, cooks, dishwashers, grocery clerks, and others who feed us all.

50   Hold a block party or street festival. Include young people and their favorite music. Do it a few years in a row, and it becomes a tradition.

51   Hold regular shared meals in parks, community centers, or churches. Make them free, so people who are hungry can participate without shame.

52   Create playful spaces and events for children and adults. Hold a dog parade.

53   Start a fab lab at a school or community college, where people can learn computer-aided design and fabrication with 3-D printing.

54   Celebrate or commemorate locally meaningful cultural milestones.

55   Get places and streets renamed after local unsung heroes and heroines.

56   Paint or commission murals that tell the unique stories of your place.

57   Hold open mics.

58   Open a space for live music, or support an existing one.

59   Create a theatrical production based on a story circle.

60   Build a free tiny neighborhood library.

61   Convene a book club.

62   Open a folk school where people can teach and learn the skills, cultures, and history of your community.

Build Your Local Economy

63   Grow local, shop local, share local. Avoid e-commerce and corporate chains.

64   Support local artists and musicians instead of watching television, Hollywood movies, or out-of-town acts.

65   Insist that institutions—public and private—that operate in your community are responsive to local aspirations. Question their legitimacy if they aren't.

66   Create a licensed kitchen incubator where people can process their favorite salsa or soup to sell.

67   Create a business incubator, with training, mentors, and office space, where people can try out their start-up ideas and collaborate.

68   Resist big-box stores.

69   Start a food hub to distribute locally grown or processed foods to restaurants, schools, and other buyers.

70 Encourage retiring business owners to sell their businesses to their workers, and help the workers form cooperatives.

71 Find creative ways for your community to help finance co-ops and local business start-ups. Urge your credit union to finance cooperatives. Consider running for the credit union board.

72 Launch a state bank like North Dakota's.

73 Encourage your library to loan out tools, bicycles, and clothes for job interviews, and to offer free Wi-Fi and heritage seeds.

74 Join a time bank, or start one, to exchange services.

75 Start a "buy nothing" Facebook page, where people can give stuff away.

76 Link sellers—like farmers and artists—with buyers via farmers' markets, craft markets, or online spaces.

77 Create community-owned electricity generation, such as solar or wind power.

78 Start community gardens and farms.

79 Create a training program on how to start a worker-owned cooperative or retail co-op.

80 Create a business to install raised-bed gardens in people's yards, in school yards, and in parks.

81 Hold seasonal swaps of children's clothes, adult clothes, and recreational gear.

82 Form urban-rural alliances for food distribution, work exchanges, cultural exchanges, and fun.

Build Power

83 Learn and teach the skills of working together, making decisions together, facilitation, mediation, and circle processes—techniques that allow groups of people to be creative and effective together, and to resolve conflicts.

84 Lift up the peacemakers, the healers, the worker bees. Acknowledge and praise them publically, especially those who get stuff done behind the scenes.

85 Run for school board or other local office. Nominate and support others who share your values.

86 Find out the mechanics of voting and ballot access, and make sure both are fair.

87 Pay attention to outside entities that are looking to exploit or privatize the commons and resources of your area, and sound the alarm.

88 Acknowledge and support the risk takers who stand up to exclusion, violence, and exploitation.

89 Crunch local government data on the impacts of policies on the well-being of various groups of people, the environment, and the community as a whole. Share with advocacy groups, journalists, and/or the public.

90 With your neighbors, prepare for natural disasters and other emergencies. Structure plans around the needs of the most vulnerable.

91 Learn about police practices in your community: Are people of color or immigrants disproportionately stopped, arrested, prosecuted, and sentenced? Are police confiscating property, or is people's inability to pay fines resulting in extended prison time? What is the mechanism for civilian oversight?

92 Start a hyper-local Facebook page or blog for issues and forums.

93 Tell your story via your own podcast.

94 Begin by "doing for ourselves," creating the world we want to live in. Don't wait for permission.

95 Gather others for study circles to deepen understanding about the issues facing your community, this moment in history, and prospects for change.

96 Hold forums to set community priorities, and then invite elected officials to respond to your agenda. Ask for commitments and report-backs.

97 Introduce participatory budgeting: Work with elected officials to create parts of the city or county budget. Get each neighborhood to define its priorities.

98 Have visioning sessions, "Imagine [your neighborhood or city]," where you meet to discuss not what's gone wrong, but what you want to create.

99 Sponsor election debates; the people who are most marginalized should moderate and ask the most questions.

100 Advocate for walkable and bike-able corridors or lanes.

101 Start a community radio station, using the airwaves or the Internet.

Notes

PROLOGUE: A BIG REVOLUTION AT A SMALL SCALE

1. Paul Buchheit, "Overwhelming Evidence that Half of America is In or Near Poverty," Alternet, http://www.alternet.org/economy/overwhelming-evidence-half -america-or-near-poverty, accessed June 3, 2016.

INTRODUCTION: WE THE PEOPLE LOVE THIS PLACE

1. Wikipedia, "1954 Guatemalan coup d'état," https://en.wikipedia.org /wiki/1954_Guatemalan_coup_d%27%C3%A9tat, accessed June 3, 2016.

2. Martin Luther King Jr., "Beyond Vietnam," http://kingencyclopedia.stanford .edu/encyclopedia/documentsentry/doc_beyond_vietnam/, accessed June 3, 2016.

CHAPTER 1: FIRE, COAL, AND CLIMATE IN MONTANA

1. The Center for Media and Democracy, "Gateway Pacific Terminal," Source-Watch, http://www.sourcewatch.org/index.php/Gateway_Pacific_Terminal, accessed June 3, 2016; Washington State Department of Ecology, "Environmental Review Gateway Pacific Terminal at Cherry Point Proposal," http://www.ecy.wa.gov /geographic/gatewaypacific/, accessed June 3, 2016.

2. Alan Yuhas, "Scientists: Air Pollution Led to More than 5.5 Million Premature Deaths in 2013," The Guardian, February 12, 2016, https://www.theguardian.com /environment/2016/feb/12/air-pollution-deaths-india-china, accessed July 14, 2016.

CHAPTER 2: ANOTHER WAY OF RANCHING

1. "Surface Mining Control and Reclamation Act of 1977," Wikipedia, https:// en.wikipedia.org/wiki/Surface_Mining_Control_and_Reclamation_Act_of_1977, accessed June 3, 2016.

2. Savory Institute, "Holistic Management: Portfolio of Scientific Findings," http://savory.global/assets/docs/evidence-papers/portfolio-of-findings.pdf, accessed June 3, 2016.

3. United Nations Convention to Combat Desertification, "Desertification," UN News Center, http://www.un.org/en/events/desertificationday/background.shtml, accessed June 3, 2016.

CHAPTER 3: THE RANCHERS AND NATIVE PEOPLE
RESISTING THE OTTER CREEK MINE

1. B. D. Hong and E. R. Slatick, "Carbon Dioxide Emission Factors for Coal," http://www.eia.gov/coal/production/quarterly/co2_article/co2.html, accessed June 3, 2016; originally published in Energy Information Administration, Quarterly Coal Report, January–April 1994, DOE/EIA-0121(94/Q1) (Washington, DC, August 1994), 1–8.

2. Calculated by the author from figures in U.S. Environmental Protection Agency, Office of Transportation and Air Quality, EPA420-F-08-024, "Average Annual Emissions and Fuel Consumption for Gasoline-Fueled Passenger Cars and Light Trucks," October 2008, https://www3.epa.gov/otaq/consumer/420f08024.pdf, accessed June 3, 2016.

CHAPTER 4: A NORTH DAKOTA RESERVATION
WHERE FRACKING RULES

1. Department of Mineral Resources, North Dakota Industrial Commission, "North Dakota Annual Oil Production," https://www.dmr.nd.gov/oilgas/stats/annualprod.pdf, accessed June 3, 2016.

2. Tim McDonnell, "How 3,500 Voters in North Dakota Could Put the Brakes on America's Biggest Fracking Boom," *Mother Jones* magazine, https://www.motherjones.com/environment/2014/11/north-dakota-oil-reservation-election, accessed June 3, 2016.

3. Executive Office of the President of the United States, "National Drug Control Strategy," https://www.whitehouse.gov/sites/default/files/ndcs 2014.pdf, accessed June 3, 2016.

4. Sierra Crane-Murdoch, "The Other Bakken Boom: A Tribe Atop the Nation's Biggest Oil Play," Property and Environment Research Center, November 28, 2012, www.perc.org/articles/other-bakken-boom, accessed July 15, 2016.

CHAPTER 5: NO FRACKING WAY TURTLE MOUNTAIN

1. U.S. Energy Information Administration, "Annual Coal Report 2014, Table 18," http://www.eia.gov/coal/annual/pdf/table18.pdf, accessed June 3, 2016.

2. David Erickson, "Report: 64K Jobs in Montana Depend on Outdoor Recreation on Public Lands," Independent Record: Helena Local News, http://helenair.com/news/local/report-k-jobs-in-montana-depend-on-outdoor-recreation-on/article_33e060c8-6cec-5f15-8eb7-edbab0c7e2c8.html, accessed June 3, 2016.

3. "Full Results of New York Times/CBS News Poll on the Environment," *The New York Times*, November 30, 2015; poll conducted November 18–22, 2015; http://www.nytimes.com/interactive/2015/11/30/science/earth/01poll-document.html, accessed June 3, 2016.

4. Bruce Drake, "How Americans View the Top Energy and Environmental Issues," Pew Research Center RSS, January 15, 2015, http://www.pewresearch.org/key-data-points/environment-energy-2/, accessed June 3, 2016.

CHAPTER 6: THE MAKING OF THE RUST BELT

1. Drew DeSilver, "Despite Recent Shootings, Chicago Nowhere near U.S. 'Murder Capital,'" Pew Research Center RSS, July 14, 2014, http://www.pewresearch.org/fact-tank/2014/07/14/despite-recent-shootings-chicago-nowhere-near-u-s-murder-capital/, accessed June 3, 2016.

2. Sarahtr, "More than 1.3 Million in Chicago Metro Area Live in Poverty," *Chicago Sun-Times*, September 18, 2014, http://chicago.suntimes.com/politics/more-than-1-3-million-in-chicago-metro-area-live-in-poverty/, accessed June 3, 2016.

CHAPTER 7: GROWING POWER IN CHICAGO

1. J. J. Keller & Associates, Inc., "Food Industry Injury Rates 60 Percent Higher than Other Trades, Study Shows," July 20, 2015, http://www.jjkeller.com/shop/content_category_Workplace Safety_article_Food-industry-injury-rates-60-percent-higher-than-other-trades-study-shows*072015_10151_-1_10551, accessed June 3, 2016.

CHAPTER 9: THE DETROITERS WHO ARE REDEFINING PROSPERITY

1. Daniel Fisher, "America's Most Dangerous Cities: Detroit Can't Shake No. 1 Spot," *Forbes*, October 29, 2015, http://www.forbes.com/sites/danielfisher/2015/10/29/americas-most-dangerous-cities-detroit-cant-shake-no-1-spot/#597d2d2c12c8, accessed June 3, 2016.

2. Josh Sanburn, "This Is the Poorest Big City in the U.S.," *Time*, September 17, 2015, http://time.com/4039249/detroit-poverty-rate-census/, accessed June 3, 2016.

CHAPTER 10: DR. GARCIA, GUNSHOT WOUNDS,
AND A PLEA FOR JOBS IN CINCINNATI

1. J. D. Harrison, "Who Actually Creates Jobs: Start-ups, Small Businesses or Big Corporations?," *The Washington Post*, April 25, 2013, https://www.washingtonpost.com/business/on-small-business/who-actually-creates-jobs-start-ups-small-businesses-or-big-corporations/2013/04/24/d373ef08-ac2b-11e2-a8b9-2a63d75b5459_story.html, accessed June 3, 2016.

2. Andrew Dugan, "Americans Still More Confident in Small vs. Big Business," Gallup.com, July 6, 2015, http://www.gallup.com/poll/183989/americans-confident-small-big-business.aspx, accessed June 3, 2016.

3. Dennis Jacobe, "Americans' Confidence in Banks Falls to Record Low," Gallup.com, June 27, 2012, http://www.gallup.com/poll/155357/Americans-Confidence-Banks-Falls-Record-Low.aspx, accessed June 3, 2016.

CHAPTER 11: THE UNION MOVEMENT'S HAIL MARY PASS

1. Zaid Jilani, "REPORT: The American Middle Class Was Built by Unions and It Will Decline Without Them," *Think Progress*, Center for American Progress, September 5, 2011, http://thinkprogress.org/economy/2011/09/05/311831/american-middle-class-organized-labor/, accessed July 14, 2016.

2. Alison Lingane, "As Boomers Retire, Millions of Small Businesses Will Change Hands. Can We Keep Them Local?" *YES! Magazine*, November 13, 2015, http://www.yesmagazine.org/new-economy/as-boomers-retire-millions-of-small-businesses-will-change-hands-can-we-keep-them-local-20151113, accessed July 14, 2016.

CHAPTER 13: APPALACHIA'S COALFIELDS EXTRACTION

1. "Why Poverty Persists in Appalachia: An Interview with Cynthia M. Duncan," *Frontline*, December 29, 2005, http://www.pbs.org/wgbh/pages/frontline/countryboys/readings/duncan.html, accessed June 3, 2016.

2. Brad Plumer, "Here's Why Central Appalachia's Coal Industry Is Dying," *The Washington Post*, November 4, 2014, https://www.washingtonpost.com/news/wonk/wp/2013/11/04/heres-why-central-appalachias-coal-industry-is-dying/, accessed June 3, 2016.

3. Tanner Hosterberg, "Budget Signed by President Clears Way for Federal Prison in Letcher County," WYMT-TV, December 18, 2015, http://www.wymt.com/content/news/Budget-signed-by-president-clears-way-for-federal-prison-in-Letcher-County-362999401.html, accessed July 15, 2016.

4. Sylvia Ryerson, "Speak Your Piece: Prison Progress?" *The Daily Yonder*, February 13, 2013, http://www.dailyyonder.com/speak-your-piece-prison-progress/2013/02/20/5651/, accessed July 15, 2016.

5. Panagioti Tsolkas, "Federal Prison in Letcher County Wrong for Region, Environment, Prisoners," *Lexington Herald-Leader*, August 31, 2015, http://www/kentucky.com/opinion/op-ed/article42610920.html, accessed June 3, 2016.

6. U.S. Energy Information Administration, Independent Statistics and Analysis, "Power Sector Employment Declines, except for Renewable Electricity Generators," December 19, 2014, http://www.eia.gov/todayinenergy/detail.cfm?id=19271, accessed June 3, 2016.

7. Rabla Ferroukhi et al., "Renewable Energy and Jobs: Annual Review 2015," International Renewable Energy Agency (IRENA), 2015, www.irena.org/Document Download/Publications/IRENA_RE_Jobs_Annual_Review_2015.pdf, accessed July 15, 2016.

8. "The State of Obesity in Kentucky," State Obesity Data, Rates, and Trends: The State of Obesity, a project of the Trust for America's Health and the Robert Wood Johnson Foundation, http://stateofobesity.org/states/ky, accessed June 3, 2016.

CHAPTER 14: GREENSBORO'S BATTLE OVER STORY

1. Fania Davis, "Truth and Reconciliation at Work: How These Commissions Help Heal Wounds from Racial Injustice," *YES! Magazine* 74, Make It Right issue (Summer 2015): 45.

2. Jill E. Williams, "Legitimacy and Effectiveness of a Grassroots Truth and Reconciliation Commission," *Law and Contemporary Problems* 72, no. 143 (Spring 2009), Scholarship.law.duke.edu/cgi/viewcontent.cgi?article=1523&context=lcp, accessed July 16, 2016.

3. Cited in Elizabeth Stanley, "Evaluating the Truth and Reconciliation Commission," *Journal of Modern Africa Studies* 39, no. 3 (September 2001): 525–546, Center.theparentscircle.org/images/f93ce18beels14901b39ef76238aba4f9.pdf, accessed July 16, 2016.

4. "Greensboro, North Carolina (NC) Poverty Rate Data, Information about Poor and Low Income Residents," http://www.city-data.com/poverty/poverty -Greensboro-North-Carolina.html, accessed June 3, 2016.

CHAPTER 15: RESTORATIVE JUSTICE
AND THE HARRISONBURG POLICE

1. Sophia Kerby, "The Top 10 Most Startling Facts About People of Color and Criminal Justice in the United States," Center for American Progress, March 13, 2012, https://www.americanprogress.org/issues/race/news/2012/03/13/11351/the-top-10 -most-startling-facts-about-people-of-color-and-criminal-justice-in-the-united -states/, accessed July 17, 2016.

2. Sharon Leslie Morgan and Thomas Norman DeWolf, "His Ancestors Were Slave Traders and Hers Were Slaves. What They Learned About Healing from a Roadtrip," *YES! Magazine* 74 (May 23, 2015): 18, http://www.yesmagazine.org/issues /make-it-right/healing-historys-wound, accessed July 17, 2016.

3. Craig Fischer, "Legitimacy and Procedural Justice: A New Element of Police Leadership. A Report by the Police Executive Research Forum (PERF)." March 2014, http://www.policeforum.org/assets/docs/Free_Online_Documents/Leadership /legitimacy and procedural justice - a new element of police leadership.pdf, accessed July 17, 2016.

CHAPTER 16: NEWARK AND THE PEOPLE WHO LOVE IT

1. "Crime in America 2015: Top 10 Most Dangerous Cities Over 200,000," Law Street, http://lawstreetmedia.com/crime-america-2015-top-10-dangerous-cities -200000-2/, accessed June 3, 2016.

CHAPTER 17: ITHACA'S STORIES OF RACE

1. "Ithaca Population and Demographics," AreaConnect, based on 2000 US Census data, http://ithaca.areaconnect.com/statistics.htm, accessed June 3, 2016.

2. Richard Rothstein, "Segregation Has Never Really Ended: The Link Between

Housing and Education," *Hillman: On the Issues*, May 6, 2014, http://www.hillman foundation.org/sites/default/files/SHF_OnTheIssues_140506_Rothstein.pdf, accessed June 3, 2016.

CHAPTER 18: DALLAS AT CHRISTMAS AND A SYRIAN FAMILY

1. Avi Selk, "A Weekend of Angst over Islam: Guns in Richardson, Marchers in Dallas and a Quiet Conversation in Irving," The Scoop Blog, *Dallas Morning News*, December 12, 2015, http://thescoopblog.dallasnews.com/2015/12/a-weekend-of -angst-over-islam-guns-in-richardson-marchers-in-dallas-and-a-quiet-conver sation-in-irving.html/, accessed June 3, 2016.

CHAPTER 19: CHILDBIRTH AND TRANSCENDENCE

1. Vincent J. Felitti et al., "Relationship of Childhood Abuse and Household Dysfunction to Many of the Leading Causes of Death in Adults," *American Journal of Preventive Medicine* 14, no. 4, 245–258, accessed June 3, 2016.

CHAPTER 20: MOAB—A BRIDGE

1. Jonathan Clayton, "Worldwide Displacement Hits All-time High as War and Persecution Increase," UNHCR News, http://www.unhcr.org/news/latest /2015/6/558193896/worldwide-displacement-hits-all-time-high-war-persecution increase.html, accessed June 3, 2016.

Acknowledgments

I could not have made this journey without the support and help of people I met throughout my four and a half months on the road. And I couldn't have started off without the staff, board, and supporters of YES! *Magazine.* YES! gave me the flexibility to be out of the office, a network to draw on for leads and hospitality, and support for my travels. Stephen Miller, now YES! senior editor, created a website to tell the stories from the road as I traveled, complete with an interactive map, and acted as my main editor and liaison. Christa Hillstrom, YES! senior editor, introduced me to Cedar Gillette and Christa Monette, who told me about the extraordinary things happening in Fort Berthold and on the Turtle Mountain Reservation. I especially want to thank YES! executive director Fran Korten, who supported my plan to make this trip and write this book. Fran and David Korten have been extraordinary colleagues since we founded YES! and have influenced my understanding of the world in countless ways.

Knowing Akaya Windwood has been life changing. On more than one occasion, including when I decided to take this trip, her clarity and wisdom have helped me understand what I needed to do.

I also want to thank Kate Ahvakana and Toma Villa for their extraordinary painting of my camper, Roger van Gelder for getting my truck prepared mechanically to make the trip, and my kids, Martha and Alex van Gelder, for always supporting me.

I am grateful to Steve Piersanti and the staff at Berrett-Koehler for their support for this book project; it is truly wonderful to work with a publisher that is so ethical and professional. I thank Paul Dunn for the photograph of the truck and me, and *YES! Magazine*'s Tracy Loeffelholz Dunn and Jennifer Lufton for consulting on the cover design.

The following people read all or parts of the book and gave me helpful insights and feedback: Charlotte Ashlock, Dee Axelrod, Amity Bacon, Peter Block, Britt Bravo, Tracey Briggs, David Korten, Fran Korten, Steve Piersanti, George Price, Robin Simons, Katie Vastola, Ed Whitfield, and Akaya Windwood.

Finally, the trip and this book wouldn't have been possible without all the people quoted in the book—I am grateful to you for your time. The following people hosted me, showed me around their community, shared their knowledge, and introduced me to other people I needed to know: Ada Smith, Alaina Buffalo Spirit, Christa Monette, Claudia S. Brown, Cristina Turino, David Orr, Ed Whitfield, Elaine Heath, Elizabeth Barnett, Fred Carter, George Siemon, Gregg MacDonald, Halima Cassells, James Lamar Gibson, Dr. Jifunza Wright Carter, Jim Embry, Jim Webb, Joan Kresich, Kathy Evans, Kristen Barker, Keith Aziz Hamilton, Lama Tsomo, Linn DeNesti, Ma Teresa Lomeli Penman, Madhu Suri Prakash, Matthew Smith, Maura Stephens, Megan Hollingsworth, Nicolle and Thomas Gonzales, Kim Mitchell, Kim Sherobbi, Pam McMichael, Paul Wheaton,

Paulette Moore, Peter Block, Richard Feldman, Roodline Volcy, Sara Hess, Tawana Petty, Tim Allanbrook, and Todd Rusk.

I also want to thank the following people for sharing their ideas and insights with me and connecting me to others: Adela Nieves, Aisha Ellis, Alexander Gibson, Alexis Bonogofsky, Andrew Kang Bartlett, Anthony Schuman, Bayard P. Love, Betty Knighton, Bill Moyer, Brett Jones, Bryce Detroit, Burt Lauderdale, Carl Stauffer, Carol Marsh, Cedar Gillette, Charline Watts, Cheri Bryant Hamilton, Chris Brown, Dante Garcia, Colin Lauderdale, Dara Cooper, David Anderson Hooker, Elandria Williams, Ellen Vera, Erika Allen, Fania Davis, Flequer Vera, Freddy Lane, Garlin Gilchrist II, George Price, Godfrey L. Simmons Jr., Jackson Koeppel, Jacob Hundt, Jeff Cohen, Jeff Furman, Jeff Smith, Jewell Praying Wolf James, Jo An Gaines, Jocelyn Campbell, Jodie Evans, Jodie Geddes, Joyce Johnson, Julia Putnam, Kara Kaufman, Kat Gjovik, Kaye Kirsch, Kurt Boshart, Laura Gwen Haber, Lil Erikson, Liz Walker, Lucianne Siers, Marc McCord, Marnie Thompson, Mary Louise Frampton, Matt Turino, Nick Engelfried, Omavi Shukur, Prairie Rose Seminole, Reuben George, Reverend Joan Ross, Richard Conlin, Richard Westheimer, Rebecca Kemble, Sarah Chalmers, Shea Howell, Steve Charter, Ted Howard, Grace Lee Boggs, Trevor Phillips, Tribal Chairman Richard McCloud, Victor Garcia, Walter Brueggemann, Wayne Curtis, Myrtle Denise Thompson, Wes Magruder, Will Allen, William Copeland, and Zoltan Grossman.

And I want to especially thank my fiancée, Dee Axelrod, for her steadfast support during the long months I was traveling and writing, for sharing her wisdom and insights on the topics in this book, and for her invaluable feedback on the manuscript. I can't imagine this project could have been possible without her support.

Index

A "p" following a page number indicates a photograph.

About the Author

Sarah van Gelder is cofounder and editor-at-large of *YES! Magazine*.

In August 2015, Sarah embarked on a road trip to Native reservations, Rust Belt cities, small Appalachian towns, and ranching communities. This book, *The Revolution Where You Live*, is the story of that trip.

She also writes columns and articles published in *YES! Magazine* and YESMagazine.org, *Huffington Post*, the *Guardian*, *Alternet*, the *Christian Science Monitor*, *Truthout*, the *Dallas Morning News*, and elsewhere, and speaks internationally and as a guest on radio and television programs across the country.

Sarah led the development of *YES!* from a scrappy start-up, operating out of a basement in 1996, to a publication that is nationally recognized for leading-edge solutions to the major ecological and human challenges of our times. The magazine has won national awards for its leadership in covering such topics as the cooperative economy, mass incarceration, neighborhood sustainability, and personal resilience.

She has interviewed Pete Seeger, George Shultz, Fania and Angela Davis, Muhammad Yunus, Desmond Tutu, Naomi Klein, Ralph Nader, Tom Goldtooth, and others. She is editor of the books *Sustainable Happiness: Live Simply, Live Well, Make a Difference* and *Occupy Wall Street and the 99 Percent Movement*, both with Berrett-Koehler Publishers.

Sarah lives on the reservation of the Suquamish Tribe, where, along with a tribal elder, she founded an organization to combat anti-Indian hostility. As cochair of that group, she collaborated with the tribe to win the return to the Suquamish of the land where Chief Seattle once lived. She currently serves on the board of the tribally chartered Suquamish Foundation and participates with the tribe's canoe family on the annual canoe journey.

She has also been a radio and television producer, and she cofounded one of the country's first cohousing communities. Sarah has lived in China, India, and Central America. She is the mother of two young adults.

Berrett–Koehler
Publishers

Berrett-Koehler is an independent publisher dedicated to an ambitious mission: *connecting people and ideas to create a world that works for all.*

We believe that to truly create a better world, action is needed at all levels—individual, organizational, and societal. At the individual level, our publications help people align their lives with their values and with their aspirations for a better world. At the organizational level, our publications promote progressive leadership and management practices, socially responsible approaches to business, and humane and effective organizations. At the societal level, our publications advance social and economic justice, shared prosperity, sustainability, and new solutions to national and global issues.

A major theme of our publications is "Opening Up New Space." Berrett-Koehler titles challenge conventional thinking, introduce new ideas, and foster positive change. Their common quest is changing the underlying beliefs, mindsets, institutions, and structures that keep generating the same cycles of problems, no matter who our leaders are or what improvement programs we adopt.

We strive to practice what we preach—to operate our publishing company in line with the ideas in our books. At the core of our approach is stewardship, which we define as a deep sense of responsibility to administer the company for the benefit of all of our "stakeholder" groups: authors, customers, employees, investors, service providers, and the communities and environment around us.

We are grateful to the thousands of readers, authors, and other friends of the company who consider themselves to be part of the "BK Community." We hope that you, too, will join us in our mission.

A BK Currents Book

This book is part of our BK Currents series. BK Currents books advance social and economic justice by exploring the critical intersections between business and society. Offering a unique combination of thoughtful analysis and progressive alternatives, BK Currents books promote positive change at the national and global levels. To find out more, visit **www.bkconnection.com**.